DATE DUE			
			ALESCO

The World of Mary Cassatt

The World of Mary Cassatt

illustrated with photographs

BY ROBIN McKOWN

THOMAS Y. CROWELL COMPANY   NEW YORK

Women of America
MILTON MELTZER, EDITOR

L.C. Card 77-139106
ISBN 0-690-90274-3

1   2   3   4   5   6   7   8   9   10

For Dorothy Thompson Worden,
WHOSE INSTINCTS ARE AS PURE
AND UNCOMPROMISING AS THE
SUBJECT OF THIS BOOK

Acknowledgments

A great many people, in America and France, contributed to this book in one way or another—to all of whom I wish here to express my gratitude. I would like to give special thanks to Dr. Frederick A. Sweet, former curator of American painting and sculpture at the Art Institute of Chicago, for permission to make use of background facts in his work, *Miss Mary Cassatt;* to Mrs. Dorothy Thompson Worden, an excellent artist herself, for her invaluable advice and research assistance; to Mrs. Adelyn D. Breeskin, curator of contemporary art at the Smithsonian Institution, for graciously passing on information garnered in her own long study of Mary Cassatt; to Angela Russell of the Parke-Bernet Galleries, Inc., for making available records on Mary Cassatt's works; to Ann Kuss of Penn Central, for information about Alexander Cassatt; to Miss Christine Jones of the Pennsylvania Academy of the Fine Arts; Henry G. Gardiner, assistant curator of paintings, at the Philadelphia Museum of Art; Mrs. Alice L. Wright of the Cleveland Museum of Art; John K. Howatt, associate curator in charge of American paintings and sculpture, at the Metropolitan Museum of Art; Mary L. Jameson of the Museum of Fine Arts, Boston; Joseph J. Rishell, assistant curator of painting and sculpture, at the Art Institute of Chicago—all of whom were helpful and cooperative; and to the staffs of the New York Public Library in New York City, the Bibliothèque Nationale in Paris, and the Corning (New York) Public Library, who were especially obliging in tracing rare and out-of-print books for my use.

—ROBIN MCKOWN

Contents

Illustrations

The World of Mary Cassatt

I

A Child of Two Worlds

Mary Cassatt's life was a series of paradoxes.

She was a product of conventional nineteenth-century American society, which decreed that woman's place was in the home, but she defied that society by seeking a professional career as an artist.

She has been called "America's First Lady of Art," but she spent most of her life in France, and the French esteemed her as an artist of great merit long before her own country recognized her.

Although France gave her artistic inspiration, fame, and admirers, her first loyalties were always to America. With all her years abroad, she never ceased being American to the core.

She painted mothers and children with a freshness and realism that has rarely been equaled, but she never married and had no children of her own.

Prim and proper and conventional in her personal life, she championed the French Impressionist painters at a time when they were being denounced as radicals and revolutionaries. Her name will always be linked with these Impressionists. She exhibited with them, bought their paintings, and insisted that her friends do likewise. But she was never an Impressionist herself.

The Impressionists presented a startling paradox, too. In their personal lives, nearly all of them suffered cruel hardships. Yet they painted perhaps the most joyous paintings in the history of art, filled with light, color, and the subtle and changing beauties of nature. They portrayed the simple pleasures of ordinary people. Sooner or later tragedy touched all Mary Cassatt's colleagues, even the aristocratic Edgar Degas, who was closer to her than any of the others.

These artists preferred painting to talking about their work. They let their pictures speak for themselves. Almost unanimously, they left to art scholars the task of analysis or criticism or devising theories about what they had done. This is not a book of art criticism either, but is about people who happened to be artists—especially the Philadelphia spinster Mary Cassatt, whose daring use of color and strong lines set her apart from her timid American contemporaries and placed her on terms of equality with the most advanced French artists of her time.

When Mary Cassatt was born on May 23, 1844, the United States was still a new country. A mere sixty-eight years had passed since the Declaration of Independence. John Tyler, one of the least known American presidents, was in the White House. There was a rising tension between the free states of the north and the slave states of the south. Law-abiding Quakers of Mary's native Pennsylvania were active in the illegal Underground Railroad, helping southern slaves escape to freedom. It would still be four years before the discovery of gold in California.

The Cassatt family traced its ancestry back to one Jacques Cossart, a sixteenth-century French Huguenot who had left Catholic France in search of religious freedom. He went first to the Palatinate in Germany, then on to the New World, and settled in New Amsterdam, present-day New York. There he became a miller and prospered. One of his descendants, Francis Cossart, served in Congress during the American Revolution and afterward helped frame Pennsylvania's first state constitution.

Eventually the Cossarts changed the family name to Cassat, accented on the last syllable. Robert Cassatt, Mary's father, added the last *t* to their name. After she moved to France, Mary Cassatt sometimes referred to her "Gallic" ancestry, though in fact she had less than two per cent "French blood." For the rest, she was a mixture of Scotch, Irish, and Dutch.

Her mother had seven children, of whom two died within a month of their birth. Of the five who survived, Mary Stevenson Cassatt was the next to youngest. She was seven years younger than Lydia, her only sister, and five years younger than her oldest brother, Alexander Johnston

Cassatt. Robert, named after his father, was two years Mary's senior. The youngest of the family, Joseph Gardner Cassatt, was born when Mary was five. The family always called him Gardner.

According to one authority, the Cassatts were persons of such marked individuality, they were referred to by their friends and neighbors as "Cassatturated."

Their father was a broker and real estate agent, and moderately prosperous. But he did not think making money should be an end in itself. He took pride in his knowledge of politics, literature, and art. Mrs. Cassatt, a shy and reserved woman except in the intimacy of her family, was considered a scholar since she had learned French from a Parisian. This accomplishment alone marked her as exceptional. Few women had the courage or the independence to follow intellectual pursuits. Women's place was definitely in the home, and there was as yet no talk of women's rights, either to vote or to take up a professional career.

Culturally, America was at a low ebb of mediocrity in the mid-nineteenth century. No artist had appeared to rival the early portrait painters John Singleton Copley, Charles Willson Peale, and Gilbert Stuart—and John Trumbull, who came nearer than any other to being the official painter of the American Revolution. Nor could anyone compete with the huge twenty-foot canvases of Benjamin West, a native of Pennsylvania, who in fact had spent most of his life in England as royal painter to King George III.

The artists in favor were those who painted pretty, sentimental pictures, which told a touching story or pointed a moral. There were some itinerant portrait painters who roamed the country, charging so much a head, with bargain rates for students. If the likeness was flattering, their clients were satisfied. It is probably safe to say that there was more artistic merit in the women's crazy quilts of brightly colored bits of silk sewed together with intricate handstitching than in almost any of the productions of contemporary artists.

Moral standards were strict, overlapping into intolerance. Class lines were rigid. The teachings of Thomas Paine and Thomas Jefferson were all but forgotten. It was all very well for the Constitution to assert that "all men were created equal," but that sentiment was not to be taken too literally. The "respectable" middle class did not associate with the lower classes, who were considered lazy and uncouth rather than underprivileged. Charity meant giving Christmas baskets to the "deserving poor" or supporting missionaries who taught Christianity to the heathen of foreign lands.

This respectable middle class, with its iron-clad rules and regulations, was the society into which Mary Cassatt was born. She would rebel against it in many ways but it was always part of her.

Her birthplace was Allegheny City, which was across the Allegheny River from Pittsburgh, and which is now part of Pittsburgh. When she was two, her father was elected mayor of Allegheny City. He served in this post for two years and then moved his family across the river to Pittsburgh.

They moved again before the end of the year to a farm called Hardwick, in the rolling hills of Lancaster County. Mr. Cassatt shortly rented a house in Philadelphia but retained Hardwick as their country home. Mary learned how to ride horseback there. Aleck, as they called her big brother Alexander, probably helped her mount and held the bridle for her. He said later she was always ready whenever he proposed a walk, a ride, or a gallop. Both of them had quick tempers, fought often, and made up quickly.

Aside from the fact of her temper, confirmed by Alexander, almost nothing is known of Mary Cassatt's personality as a child. She was never one to talk about her early childhood, possibly because on the whole she remembered it as rather boring. Little girls of her time and class did not have much fun or freedom. They could not romp and play the tomboy like poor children. Boys and girls alike were expected to be neat, obedient, and respectful to their elders, and to be "seen and not heard" at the dinner table. The father was the master of the household and his word was law.

What perhaps made Mary's childhood livelier than most was Mr. Cassatt's penchant for moving from one place to another. Usually there were business reasons involved. He always managed to sell properties at more than he paid for them. It also seems true that he was a restless man who thrived on change.

Philadelphia became Mary's home when she was five, with Hardwick for vacations. She always thought of herself as a Philadelphian, though her total residence in that city covered only a small span of years.

When she was seven, her father suddenly decided to take the whole family to Europe for an indefinite stay. Like many Americans, he looked to the Old World yearningly, as a symbol of culture. It had all the advantages America lacked—magnificent architecture, splendid museums, superior schools, the finest in concerts and theaters. Undoubtedly he thought the trip would be good for the children. Though he was not a rich man, he did not have to worry about the cost. Living in Europe was fantastically cheap—for Americans.

By the autumn of 1851, they were installed in the Hotel

Continental in Paris—Mr. and Mrs. Cassatt, Lydia, Alexander, Robert, Mary, and the baby, Gardner. They were still at the Continental on December 2, 1852, when Napoleon Bonaparte's nephew, Louis Napoleon, who had been president of France's Second Republic, made himself Emperor of France in a bloodless coup. Mr. Cassatt, who had been out for a walk, came back to the hotel and announced the news to his family with the words, "Well, Louis's done it!"

As Napoleon III, the new emperor would strive mightily to bring France to the foreground of European powers, industrially and militarily. For the common people of France, his twenty-year dictatorship would mean oppression and hardship. For Americans abroad, the most striking result of the new regime would be the renovation of Paris. Wide boulevards replaced many of the ancient, narrow, crooked streets. The addition of thousands of gas lamps would give Paris the name of the City of Light.

Travel abroad was a leisurely affair in those days. American tourists weighed themselves down with mounds of trunks, wardrobes for every season, and such amenities of home comfort as silver tea sets, silk embroidered piano covers, hand-painted china, and brass candlesticks. All this luggage diminished their enthusiasm for exploring Europe, especially since the only way to travel was by train and train voyages were uncomfortable, tiring, and harassing. Consequently most foreign visitors tended to settle down in one spot, for weeks or months or longer.

Eventually the Cassatts found a furnished apartment in Paris, which was less expensive than the hotel and more homelike. The children dutifully went to French schools and with the aid of their mother learned French after a fashion. In time Mary became fluent in that language, though she never lost her American accent. Mr. Cassatt could read French newspapers but had trouble making his needs known in this foreign tongue.

After two years in Paris he was ready for a change again, and he took his family, bag and baggage, to the picturesque German university town of Heidelberg. Fourteen-year-old Alexander, who had a flair for mathematics, was placed in an excellent technical school.

An artist named Baumgartner painted a portrait of the Cassatts while they were in Heidelberg. It shows young Robert playing chess with his father, and five-year-old Gardner in a Scotch plaid suit, resting his elbow on the chess table, while Mary stands behind them. A prim and pretty little girl, she wears a long-sleeved, high-necked velvet dress. Her grey eyes are wide and observant. Her hair is braided in two tight pigtails, looped and tied with hair ribbons. Only her small, determined chin indicates that already she has a mind of her own.

After a year in Heidelberg, the Cassatts moved to Darmstadt, seventeen miles south of Frankfurt, where Alexander was enrolled in one of Germany's best technical universities. Mary's brother Robert, who had always been sickly, died in Darmstadt on May 25, 1855. Soon after this tragedy the Cassatts returned to Paris.

They found the city in a festive mood. The Paris Exposition Universelle, or World's Fair of 1855, the biggest and most impressive event of the century, was under way. Royal visitors were arriving from all over Europe. When Queen Victoria and her husband, Prince Albert, came with their royal retinue from England, a million cheering Parisians lined the streets, and flags hung from every window. The Cassatt family were among the spectators. Mary was delighted with all that pageantry.

In the words of Napoleon III, the purpose of the Fair was "to unite all Europe in one big family." It was also designed to show how France had progressed in the four years since he had proclaimed himself emperor, and, rather incidentally, how France surpassed her rivals in the arts.

A unique feature of the Fair was its exhibition of international art at the Palace of Fine Arts (Palais des Beaux-Arts). Twenty-eight nations contributed. It was hailed as "the most remarkable collection of painting and sculpture ever assembled under a single roof." Admittedly the French contribution dominated all the rest.

The Cassatts naturally took their children to this most important cultural affair. In gallery after gallery, walls were crowded with paintings up to the high, vaulted ceilings—unlike modern museums, where paintings are spaced widely apart so they can be fully viewed and appreciated. There were vast numbers of spectators. Women in hooped and ruffled skirts and fashionable flowered bonnets filed past the paintings sedately. Men in formal attire gathered in animated groups to discuss them. The Cassatt children docilely trailed after their parents. They may have watched with amusement the gestures with which the men reinforced their arguments—their way of talking with their hands looked so funny and foreign to Americans. They may have wondered what on earth anyone could find to argue about at an art exposition where all the paintings were equally impressive and framed in equally handsome gilded frames.

Had Mary understood French well enough, which is doubtful, she might have learned that visitors were debating, with great passion, the relative merits of two of the largest French exhibitors. One was J. A. D. Ingres, who had more than forty canvases on display. The other was Eugène Delacroix, who had thirty. Both Ingres and Delacroix had their champions.

"Portrait of Ingres," Heinrich Lehmann. *Courtesy of the Art Institute of Chicago.*

The paintings of Ingres had a carefully balanced composition, a statuesque immobility, and subdued coloring. Ingres stressed the importance of the lines that form the basic outline of a painting. "Draw lines, many lines," he told aspiring artists. He was a Classicist, that is, he looked to the ancient Greeks and Romans for inspiration. The Classicists were the conservatives of their time. They had the approval of the government-controlled Academy of Fine Arts (Académie des Beaux-Arts). Among them, Ingres stood out as the most masterful technician.

Delacroix was the leader of the new Romantic movement, which was in opposition to the Classicists, or Academicians. His canvases, crowded with figures, were filled with movement and action. He took his themes from Dante, Shakespeare, Milton, Goethe, Byron. A visit to Morocco had taught him new color harmonies and the poetry of the exotic. Through color, he conveyed emotion.

Ingres versus Delacroix. Classicism versus Romanticism. Line versus color. The Paris art world, which thrived on controversy, talked of little else.

The Cassatts must have also seen the works of other excellent French artists at the Fair's international exhibition. There were some lovely landscapes by Jean Baptiste Camille Corot, Charles François Daubigny, and Jean François Millet. Corot, Daubigny, and Millet were known as the Barbizon painters, since they did much of their painting in the Forest of Fontainebleau near Barbizon. Landscapes were unpopular in France in this era. These painters received little attention.

There was another French exhibitor whose works were even less popular at this time. This was Gustave Courbet, a huge, black-bearded, robust man with the air of a jovial baker. Courbet was the founder of the Realist movement. The men and women in his paintings were so lifelike they seemed ready to step from his canvases. He used vivid colors at a time when only dull ones were considered good taste. The international exhibition jury had reluctantly admitted a few of his canvases but had rejected two of Courbet's best. This made him so furious that he set up his own one-man show of some fifty paintings in a nearby hall. It is most unlikely that the Cassatts visited it. Hardly anyone did. It was thought improper for an artist to exhibit his own works.

Delacroix the Romantic, Courbet the Realist, and the Barbizon landscape painters Corot, Daubigny, and Millet received none of the prizes and awards granted at the exhibition. Their works were considered too unconventional, too revolutionary. Their fame has increased over the years. Today they are known as the precursors of modern French art, of an art movement in which Mary Cassatt would participate. If this eleven-year-old girl even then felt some kinship for these artists—especially Courbet, whom she would later revere—there is no evidence of it. If she made any comments about the paintings to her sister and brothers, they were never recorded.

By coincidence there were two visitors to the exhibition whom she would also know very well one day, both young and unknown artists. One was Camille Pissarro, a penniless young man of twenty-five, dark and swarthy with large, black, expressive eyes. His home was St. Thomas in the Virgin Islands. Against his father's wishes, Pissarro had come to Paris to seek a career as an artist, driven by a force stronger than himself. Alone, without friends or income, he already guessed he had a hard struggle ahead.

The other visitor to the exhibition, equally determined to make a career of art, was Edgar Degas, a wealthy young aristocrat descended from both French and Italian nobility. Handsome and slight in build, almost as dark as Pissarro, he already had, at the age of twenty-one, an air of disillusionment and cynicism.

Pissarro was enchanted with the color and vibrancy of the Delacroix paintings. Degas admired the strong lines of the works of Ingres. Their paths did not cross that of the Cassatts, and both would have been amazed had someone pointed out little Mary as a future colleague. In later years there would be mutual admiration and friendship between her and Pissarro. But it was Degas who changed her life.

Soon after the closing of the Paris World's Fair, the Cassatts returned to America. They had been away four years. There is no way of measuring the result of this long exposure to the cultural heritage of the Old World on the Cassatt children. That it did affect Mary, profoundly and permanently if not immediately, there is no doubt.

2

Student Days

Back in America, the Cassatts' home life was as unsettled
as ever. They lived first in West Chester, twenty-five miles
west of Philadelphia, but in 1858 moved back to Philadelphia, where Mr. Cassatt had purchased a four-story brick
house on Olive Street. Alexander enrolled in Rensselaer
Polytechnic Institute, in Troy, New York, in 1857. He re-

ceived his degree in civil engineering two years later at the age of twenty, and promptly took off for Georgia, where he worked on a railroad location job and at the same time managed a vineyard his father had purchased there. In 1860 he wrote Mr. Cassatt that Mary would want to go to Rome to study art in another three years; by that time their vineyard would be bearing, and he, Alexander, could stay home and work for them so they all could afford to go with her.

Clearly Mary had broached her wish to study art abroad sometime before. The project had already been discussed within the family circle and she had won the consent of her father and the support of her older brother. One can only speculate as to what led her to this decision.

Abraham Lincoln was elected President in 1860. The following year the country was torn asunder by the Civil War. It was no time to travel, and Mary had to abandon her dream of studying in Rome. The money for that venture was applied to the purchase of thirty-seven acres at Cheyney in Chester County, and a stone house with a Victorian-style porch on that property, which the Cassatts used as a country home. As a substitute for Rome, sixteen-year-old Mary enrolled in the Pennsylvania Academy of the Fine Arts.

The Academy, founded in 1805 by Charles Willson Peale, was the only art school in Philadelphia and one of the few in America. Located on Chestnut Street, it was housed in a building of Classical style, with broad marble steps leading up to a portico supported by two Doric columns. In the courtyard, shaded by the largest hawthorn tree in the United States, stood a replica of a statue of Ceres, the Roman goddess of agriculture. The main room inside, modeled after the Pantheon in Paris, was circular with a high dome.

Various large and somber paintings hung on the staircase and along the halls. One of them was a self-portrait of Peale painted when he was eighty-three; he stands holding up a curtain to reveal a hall in the museum of natural history that he had founded. Another was Benjamin West's allegorical painting "Death on a Pale Horse."

Between three and four hundred students were enrolled at the Academy, of which a fair proportion were girls. It was fashionable for young ladies to study art. Sketching and doing watercolors were social accomplishments, like embroidering or playing the harpsichord—aids to ensnare the young man of one's choice, or the choice of one's family, as the case might be.

The curriculum of the Academy had four sections. The largest was the antique class, which provided plaster casts of Greek and Roman sculptures, of which students were expected to make sketches. In another class students copied paintings from the Academy's permanent collection. A record still exists to show that in 1864 Mary Cassatt had a permit to copy one part of a ponderous Dutch painting called "Deliverance of Leyden." In the anatomy class lessons on "Artistic Anatomy" were given by Dr. Amos Russell Thomas, professor of anatomy at the Pennsylvania Medical University. There was also a life class, where models were provided, but this was for male students only. Not until several years after Mary left were female students allowed to sketch from models.

One drew "for better or worse," from "ancient copies and antique plaster casts," Mary Cassatt said later, describing her life at the Academy. "There was no teaching."

One of her fellow students was Thomas Eakins, one of the few contemporary American artists whom she esteemed. After he finished at the Academy, he studied in Paris for four years and then returned as an Academy instructor. He had to leave in disgrace. He believed that "Artistic Anatomy" was not enough for art students—that they should learn as much about anatomy as medical students. He was dismissed when dissected cadavers were discovered in his studio.

According to her closest friend at the Academy, Eliza Haldeman, Mary Cassatt was the best of the female students. A less talented classmate, a certain Miss Welch, once recklessly promised her "gentleman friend" that she would make a cast of his hand. Not knowing how to proceed, she called on Mary and Eliza for help. Their model was so pleased with the result of their joint effort that he called in a photographer and had the scene reenacted. Photography was still in its infancy, and to be photographed was such a thrill that Eliza described the process in great detail in a letter to her father.

They took a pose. Miss Welch and another student attacked the plaster with hammer and chisel, while Mary held the plaster dish and Eliza held a spoon. Miss Welch's friend promised each of them a print. Mary Cassatt's first sketches have vanished, but this early photograph is still in the Pennsylvania Academy archives.

This bit of fun was one bright episode in what Mary found a dreary ordeal. She did not feel she was learning anything at the Academy.

In Paris during this same period, four bearded young French artists, several years older than Mary Cassatt and far more sophisticated, were studying at the Atelier Gleyre, the studio of a Swiss art teacher named Gleyre. Their names were Claude Monet, Auguste Renoir, Alfred Sisley, and Jean-Frédéric Bazille. They were all enthusiastic, talented, and filled with the exuberance of youth. Like Mary Cassatt they were dissatisfied with their instruction, but for different reasons.

Mary Cassatt (right) and Classmates. Courtesy of the Pennsylvania Academy of the Fine Arts.

Compared to the Pennsylvania Academy of the Fine Arts, the Gleyre studio was extremely liberal. Women students could sketch from life models, alongside the men. Professor Gleyre himself was a practicing artist and felt he did his duty by his students if he showed up once or twice a week to criticize their efforts. Discipline was lax. The students played practical jokes, made up comic limericks, and were often rowdy to an extent that would never have been tolerated at the Pennsylvania Academy.

The greatest objection of the four young artists to the Gleyre studio was not the lack of discipline or the difficulty of concentrating in such an atmosphere, but the conservatism of their professor in artistic matters. As a staff member of the School of Fine Arts (École des Beaux-Arts), part of the government-controlled Académie des Beaux-Arts, he favored Academic art. The Academy still frowned on the Romanticism of Delacroix, the Realism of Courbet, and landscapes in general. The Academic painters still looked to the Greeks and Romans, rather than the world around them, for inspiration. For the most part they produced idealized scenes from ancient history or mythology, lacking in vitality and sterile in concept.

Monet and his three comrades refused to conform to Academy standards. They were all fairly advanced in their techniques. All had a definite idea as to what constituted good art. How did it happen they were still students, and under a professor for whom they had little sympathy and esteem? Except for Renoir, they were there because their parents insisted.

Of the four, Claude Monet was the most determined and self-confident. A big, husky, fiery-tempered youth, he hid his poverty by dressing in the height of fashion with lace on the cuffs of his shirt. When he was only fifteen he already had a reputation in his hometown of Le Havre, on the Normandy coast, for his clever portrait-caricatures, which he sold to his fellow townsmen at the substantial sum of twenty francs each. Eugène Boudin, an impoverished landscape painter in Le Havre, persuaded young Claude to give up this easy money for the doubtful venture of making a real artist of himself. On various excursions they took into the country, Boudin introduced him to the joys and satisfactions of painting from nature.

At the age of nineteen, Monet went to Paris for the first time, on Boudin's advice. There he made use of the facilities of the Académie Suisse, an informal studio where artists could draw from a model for a small fee. One of his colleagues was Camille Pissarro. Pissarro was as poor and unknown as when he had come from the West Indies and fallen under the spell of Delacroix at the Paris World's Fair of 1855, but his work showed the hand of a master. Ten years older than Monet, he went out of his way to give the youth the benefit of all he had learned. "Paint what you see," Pissarro advised him. "Above all, don't paint what you think people would like you to see."

After a year in Paris, Monet was called up for military duty in Algeria, where he served two years, and then he was released because of illness. His savings from his caricatures were long since exhausted. He spent the summer painting the Normandy coast and countryside with his old friend, Eugène Boudin, and a talented Dutch landscapist, Johan Barthold Jongkind.

Monet's heart was set on returning to Paris, but for this he needed his father's help. Monsieur Monet, a small storekeeper, saw no future in landscape painting and wanted his son to be a respectable Academy artist. He agreed to support him modestly in Paris, but only if he studied under a Beaux-Arts professor. With no alternative, Monet enrolled in the Atelier Gleyre. Conflict arose almost immediately. Monet drew the male model as he saw him—a homely man with large feet. Gleyre insisted he should make him as handsome as a Greek statue.

Auguste Renoir came to the Atelier Gleyre by a different route. He was born in Limoges, but soon afterward his father, a poor tailor, brought his family to Paris with the hope of finding better-paying clients. The streets of Paris were young Auguste's first school. At thirteen he was apprenticed to a porcelain manufacturer who imitated the fine products of Limoges and Sèvres. Renoir soon became so expert at adorning vases and platters with garlands and profiles of Marie Antoinette that his comrades dubbed him "Monsieur Rubens." At lunchtime he gave up eating to visit the Louvre museum, where he was entranced with the delicate coloring and frothy beauty of the eighteenth-century painters Watteau, Boucher, and Fragonard. He lost his job at seventeen, when the process of stamping designs on porcelain was perfected and hand painting was no longer needed.

An old painter named Laporte encouraged him to do his first canvas, a picture of Eve being tempted by the serpent. The painting was unveiled in the tiny Renoir apartment. The whole family sat breathless while Laporte studied it. Finally the old man announced that the youth had the making of a great artist. All he needed was the superior instruction of a Beaux-Arts professor.

For the next several years Renoir did a series of odd jobs—painting fans, decorating cafés with murals, painting religious scenes on window shades for missionaries whose churches abroad could not afford the luxury of stained-glass windows. By the time he was twenty-one he had saved enough to enroll in the Atelier Gleyre.

He was a slight, slender young man with light brown hair and beard and a mischievous expression in his eyes.

In class he wore the same old smock he had worn in his porcelain-painting days, oblivious to the mockery his apparel caused among his fellow students. Gleyre disapproved of him on principle.

"Doubtless you paint to amuse yourself, young man?" he demanded one day with heavy sarcasm.

"If it didn't amuse me, I wouldn't do it," Renoir retorted airily.

Monet overheard the remark and was delighted. Their friendship began.

Alfred Sisley, the third Gleyre student, was born in Paris of English parents. His father, a prosperous manufacturer of artificial flowers, sent him to school in London to perfect his English, hoping he would enter his business. When Alfred confessed he preferred sketching flowers to making them, Mr. Sisley arranged for him to study with an English painter. He missed the adult and civilized atmosphere of Paris and finally won his father's permission to return and study with Gleyre. A serious, reserved, black-bearded young man with a tender, romantic nature, he was more English than French in temperament.

Jean-Frédéric Bazille was the wealthiest of the four and had the most formal education. His father was a banker in Montpellier in southern France, where Bazille was born. As a youth he visited the home of an art-collector friend and saw works by Corot, Delacroix, and Courbet. It was Courbet who made the most lasting impression. "The big classic compositions are finished," he would say later. "The spectacle of daily life is much more interesting."

After he finished his secondary education, he went to Paris to study medicine to please his father, with the understanding that he could enroll in the Gleyre studio at the same time. Fashionable Paris society welcomed this charming young man—tall, slim, and handsome, with wavy blond hair and beard. He met the most important persons in the artistic, political, and musical world, but to his family he wrote that Claude Monet, "an excellent artist," was one of his two closest friends. He neglected his medical studies shamelessly and appeared only irregularly at Gleyre's studio, while in his own studio he painted what would one day be considered masterpieces.

Monet and Bazille spent their Easter vacation of 1863 at Chailly in the Forest of Fontainebleau, in the midst of the great oaks and picturesque rocks that had attracted the Barbizon painters before them. A year later, when Gleyre closed his studio because of bad eyesight, they went again to Chailly with Renoir and Sisley. Monet, the accepted leader of the four, passed on what he had learned from working with Boudin, Jongkind, and Pissarro. Gleyre's mythical beings from antiquity were forgotten, as the four young men devoted themselves to capturing the ever-changing moods and colors of skies, clouds, trees, and water.

They were the original Impressionists, though that name had not yet been invented.

It is not surprising that no news of their revolt reached the hallowed halls of the Pennsylvania Academy of the Fine Arts, where Mary Cassatt was plodding through the daily drudgery of sketching plaster casts. Far more spectacular happenings in the Paris art world passed unnoticed in America. There was, for instance, the emperor's Salon des Refusés, which took place in 1863, when Mary was in her third year at the Pennsylvania Academy.

Every year an exhibition was held in Paris by the Salon des Beaux-Arts, whose jury was composed of members of the Académie des Beaux-Arts. It was the dream of every young artist to have a painting selected by the Salon, but very few succeeded. Year after year the Salon jury showed its preference for the oldtimers and the conservatives. When on rare occasions new artists were accepted, their paintings were usually hung up high near the ceiling where no one could see them without straining. Delacroix, Courbet, and Corot, now recognized the world over as France's greatest contemporary painters, were repeatedly rejected.

The power of the Salon over the career, the fate, the very lives, of the artists can hardly be exaggerated. Unless an artist had a Salon acceptance, it was nearly impossible for him to reach an audience and sell his work. No dealer would risk handling his canvases. None of the rich collectors would buy them. He was barred from the opportunity to receive government commissions. There had long been rumblings of discontent against the arbitrary selections of the Salon jury. In 1863 the jury was even more severe than in preceding years. In all some four thousand paintings were rejected.

The protests of the rejected artists and their admirers mounted to such a crescendo that they reached the ears of Napoleon III. He stalked into the Salon galleries one day, insisted on seeing twenty or so of the works the jury had turned down, and then announced that in his opinion they were just as good as the ones that had been accepted. Thereupon he ordered that the entire four thousand be displayed in a separate exhibition, which came to be known as the Salon of the Rejected (Salon des Refusés).

Napoleon III was of course wrong. Not all the paintings the Salon turned down were worthy of attention. Still there were enough works of merit to make the exhibition worthwhile. There was a charming landscape by Camille Pissarro. There was a painting by Paul Cézanne, an intense, complex man from Aix-en-Provence in southern France, whom Renoir would later compare to a porcupine. Far from recognizing his potential genius, the Salon jury considered his works an abomination and rejected him regularly year after year. At least one American was represented—James Abbott McNeill Whistler of Massachusetts, an expatriate living in London. There was nothing by Edgar Degas. He was one of the few who felt no need of official recognition and did not yet bother to submit to the Salon or anywhere else.

A record number of visitors attended the Salon des Refusés. They came to be amused and they mocked everything they saw, the good and bad alike. In fact the painting that outraged them most, and the critics as well, was one of the best, "Picnic on the Grass" (Le Déjeuner sur l'Herbe) by Édouard Manet. Manet, a witty and urbane Parisian, was not a novice. Already he had had several paintings hung in the Salon des Beaux-Arts and was well on his way to success in the accepted channels. His painting, which shows two well-dressed men at a picnic lunch with two women, one nude and the other partially clothed, offended because the setting was modern. In the odd convention of the time, it was perfectly all right to paint nudes provided they were nymphs or goddesses. The women in this work were obviously neither.

The four young artists—Monet, Renoir, Sisley, and Bazille—rallied to Manet's support, as did Camille Pissarro. Their praise embarrassed Manet, who did not want his name linked with these unsuccessful and unconventional painters. But Manet's next picture, "Olympia," accepted by the Salon des Beaux-Arts, created an even more vehement storm of protest. This shows a nude woman lying on a divan, with a black woman servant standing beside her holding some flowers. Obviously Olympia was no more goddess or nymph than any woman one saw on the streets of Paris. She was even suspected of being a prostitute.

In the popular mind, Édouard Manet became a sort of

monster. Perfect strangers hissed him at a railroad station. Manet found himself in a predicament. He wanted to be a fashionable and conservative artist. He knew his life would be more comfortable if he were. But he found it impossible, then or ever, to limit himself to fashionable and conservative art.

In the placid gentility of American art circles, displays of deep emotion over a painting or an artist were unknown. Nor had any artist with the daring of Manet or the rebellious spirit of Monet and his colleagues appeared on the American scene. Mary Cassatt, prim and proper, neat and well-bred, finished her fourth year at the Pennsylvania Academy of the Fine Arts.

She did not graduate, since the Academy gave no degrees. She simply decided she had had enough. She had tried. She had stayed as long as was bearable in this dreary school with its mediocre instruction. She was fed up with staring at its gallery of dull paintings.

The artistic heritage she sought was not in America. Not Charles Willson Peale, that stout and stately figure in the Academy's self-portrait, nor his three talented artist sons. Not Gilbert Stuart, however admirable his portraits of George Washington. Not Benjamin West nor that more contemporary Pennslyvania Quaker, Edward Hicks, who had done more than a hundred canvases on his favorite Biblical theme, "The Peaceable Kingdom," all showing animals living together in harmony. The Lamb and the Lion might lie down together, but Mary Stevenson Cassatt could not have cared less.

What she had learned in her four years of application, she would have summed up as "Zero." Nothing.

In truth, she had made one big step. She had found out that she could not and would not be a dabbling amateur. It was not her *forte* to paint pretty watercolors so as to attract some reluctant suitor. Either she was going to be a professional artist or she would quit. Certain names of the past haunted her—Peter Paul Rubens, Rembrandt, Murillo, Titian, Frans Hals—the artists people mentioned with a touch of awe as the "Old Masters." The Academy had at least made them part of her vocabulary. She plagued and pestered her father to let her continue her studies abroad. Mr. Cassatt stalled.

The Civil War ended. Lincoln was assassinated. The Reconstruction period began. Alexander had a job-with-a-future in the Pennsylvania Railroad Company. Gardner had decided to be a banker. Lydia, still unmarried, stayed home with her parents in apparent contentment. Only Mary was proving difficult.

Her father had not minded the idea of letting her study in Rome, so long as he was convinced art was merely a passing fancy with her. He thought of himself as broad-minded. But in his thinking there was a world of difference between art as a hobby and art as a career. Like many of his class, he admired art as culture but felt that artists were not quite respectable. The idea of the daughter of a gentleman painting for a living was distinctly shocking to him. He has been quoted as telling Mary, "I would rather see you dead."

It took her more than two years to break down his resistance and persuade him to let her go to France.

3

*Paris and the
Franco-Prussian War*

She was twenty-two when she returned to Paris in 1866, a
slender and attractive American girl with a stubborn chin.
Her clothes were expensive and fashionable. Her mother
had seen to that. Mr. Cassatt had taken full precautions to
make sure she would be properly chaperoned.

Alternately she stayed with relatives or friends of the
family. Her schoolmate, Eliza Haldeman, was also studying art in Paris, and Mary spent time in her safe company.
Later Mrs. Cassatt and Lydia joined her. By proxy, she

was constantly under the watchful eyes of her worried father.

A French artist named Monsieur Charles Chaplin (no relative of the actor who later took France and the world by storm) was chosen for Mary's instructor. He was an accepted Academic painter, though perhaps, unknown even to Mary, he too had had his moments of revolt. In 1857 he had submitted to the Salon a painting of a nude, without titling her Diana or Venus or somebody else out of mythology. The painting was promptly rejected. (The Salon is the villain of this story, because of its jury's constant rejection of anything new in art. But it must be admitted that some Academic painters did charming work, within the limitations imposed on them.)

Mary did not care for her professor's smooth and luxuriant style. She did not yet know what kind of artist she wanted to be, but she was sure she did not want to paint like Monsieur Charles Chaplin. Eventually she stopped going to him. She may have tried out one or two other professors.

There is no record of how she spent her leisure time. Certainly she visited the Louvre and for the first time since her childhood gazed on the originals, not mere copies, of great European paintings. The Louvre, once a royal palace, was one of the gifts of the French Revolution to the people of France and the world. Previously only nobles and kings and very rich people had had art collections. Ordinary mortals had rarely had the chance to see them. After the Revolution these collections had been confiscated and "nationalized." By the time Mary Cassatt came to Paris, the Louvre had become, as Renoir once said, "the greatest art teacher in the world."

Back home, Alexander Cassatt became engaged to Lois Buchanan, daughter of a clergyman and a niece of former

"Art Students and Copyists at the Louvre," Winslow Homer. Courtesy of the National Gallery of Art, Washington, D.C., Rosenwald Collection.

President James Buchanan. (Snobbish high-society Philadelphians spoke of her as "that little nobody, Buchanan's niece.") Lois was a very prudish young lady who criticized her fiancé for not going to church regularly and considered deplorable his interest in the opera and the theater. Alexander wanted his future wife and his favorite sister to be friends. To oblige him, Mary wrote Lois several long and friendly letters.

In one of them, dated August 1, 1869, she described a trip through southern France, which she made with a Miss Gordon of Philadelphia. They stopped first at Mâcon, in Saône-et-Loire, but for reasons Mary did not detail were "perfectly disgusted." They went on to the resort town of Aix-les-Bains in the Savoy, but found life too "gay" for "two poor painters." (Miss Gordon, she explained, was only an amateur painter.) Their next stop was a hamlet in the Bauges Mountains, where their hosts turned over their only two beds to their American guests and slept in the barn. They considerately did not stay long.

After that, they stayed in another town in Savoy, Beaufort-sur-Doron, which they seemed to like. Mary and Miss Gordon hiked into the mountains to a spot from which they had a magnificent view of Mont Blanc, but had to wade up to their ankles in the snow. The "Savoyards" were civil, Mary said, but hard to understand since their speech was a mixture of French and Italian. All in all, it was an adventurous trip for two young women alone. Lois might well have been rather scandalized.

In Paris again, Mary sent two of her first paintings home and wrote of a third called "Mariana of the Moated Grange," based on one of Tennyson's poems. She met other American art students and exchanged sketches with two of them, Walter Gay and Alfred Q. Collins. They, too, were studying with French Academic artists, with the difference that they were not dissatisfied. A later generation of American art students would absorb eagerly every new art trend. In Mary's time they were less venturous.

Even had Mary wanted to meet with the *avant-garde* French artists, her sex and her social upbringing would have proved effective barriers. Heavily chaperoned, she could not go to the Café Guerbois, where Renoir, Bazille, Sisley, Pissarro, and the always half-starved Monet gathered in the evenings when it was too dark to paint; where the glowering Paul Cézanne occasionally put in an appearance; and where Edgar Degas showed up nearly every night to match his sardonic wit against Édouard Manet. She was as cut off from their fervent discussions as though she lived in another world.

At best she may have seen a few of their paintings which the Salon jury condescended to hang high on the gallery walls. They took Monet's "Camille," a portrait of his future wife, but rejected a far more original picture, "Summer: Women in a Garden" (L'Été, Femmes dans un Jardin). Pissarro's landscapes sometimes made the grade but were ignored by critics, as were Sisley's one acceptance and the two that Renoir had exhibited in 1864 and 1865. Manet appeared regularly, though the critics still lamented his "ugly realism."

Only a few discerning critics sensed anything outstanding in this new art. The poet Baudelaire admired the innovators and wrote in their defense, but he died in 1867 at the age of forty-six. A budding novelist, Émile Zola, a former schoolmate of Paul Cézanne, called Monet "a man in a crowd of eunuchs" in his art column in *L'Événement,* and praised Manet to the skies. The general reaction was so abusive that Zola was forced to discontinue his column.

Mary Cassatt's own art perceptions, which would later be so keen, were still undeveloped. To exhibit at the Salon seemed to her the height of glory. Whether she herself had any talent was a question mark. What she did have, and in large quantity, was determination.

The threat of war was already hovering over France in the early part of 1870. Prussian Premier Bismarck was busy scheming for a rift with France, in order to frighten the south German states into forming a united front with Prussia. Emperor Napoleon III, intent on his masked balls and other pleasures, ignored the threat. War preparations were pushed with inefficiency in France and in Prussia with thoroughness. In Philadelphia, Mr. Cassatt, more politically acute than most, became aware of the danger and ordered his daughter to come home. She obeyed reluctantly, with the knowledge that she was still very far from achieving what she had set out to do.

On August 4, 1870, Prussian soldiers crossed into Alsace and marched toward Paris, marking the beginning of the Franco-Prussian War. At Sedan, on September 1, the Prussians captured Emperor Napoleon and more than 90,000 French soldiers. When the news reached Paris, Napoleon was deposed *in absentia* and a provisional government was set up. One of the new officials was Georges Clemenceau, a brilliant young politician recently returned from America, who became mayor of Montmartre, a district in the Paris suburbs. Another was Gustave Courbet, who was named president of a commission charged with the safety of art treasures of the nation.

The war disrupted the lives of other artists in different ways. Alfred Sisley was called back to England to join his parents. Camille Pissarro fled his home in Louveciennes, west of Paris, to escape the advancing enemy. (The Germans later turned his house into a butcher shop and used his paintings as carpets to keep their feet from getting dirty.) Both Pissarro and Monet ended up in London. Neither was stirred by patriotic fervor. All they wanted was to paint in peace. When their funds were exhausted, they were saved from starvation by a lucky meeting with a Paris art dealer, Paul Durand-Ruel.

Durand-Ruel, whose father had supported the Barbizon painters when no one else would, had brought most of his stock of paintings to London for the duration. Young and courageous, he realized that the works of these two obscure artists had great value. He began to buy up their paintings at 200 to 300 francs each, more money than either had received before. Later Monet and Pissarro would introduce Paul Durand-Ruel to their colleagues. For a long time he was the savior of all of them.

Paul Cézanne, also unmoved by war fever, returned to his home in Aix-en-Provence, then evaded military service by moving to L'Estaque a few miles away. No one bothered him there. Renoir found the war stupid but nonetheless enlisted. He was assigned to the cavalry, though he had never ridden a horse, and sent to Bordeaux, where not a shot was fired.

Bazille was in Montpellier when the war broke out. With his country in peril, he put aside his painting and accepted a commission in a regiment of Zouaves. He was killed in November in a retreat at Beaune-la-Rolande. Over the past years he had repeatedly helped Monet when he was desperate, and he had shared his studio with Renoir and other less fortunate artists. As an artist himself, he had acquired a spontaneity and ease of expression that rivaled Renoir's and the same intimate feeling for nature as Pissarro and Monet. He was just beginning to be confident of his own skills.

Edgar Degas served in the artillery of the National

Guard in Paris. His company was commanded by a former classmate, Henri Rouart, a painter and collector himself. The friendship that developed lasted the rest of their lives.

Édouard Manet also joined the Paris National Guard, but sent his family south to the Pyrenees for safety. A loyal disciple, a young woman named Berthe Morisot who was an artist of great ability herself, also stayed in Paris.

On September 19 the Prussians began a siege of Paris. "Only children and sick people now have milk," Manet wrote his wife on October 1. On December 2, he told her, "We eat horseflesh when we can get it—cats, dogs, and rats are now sold in the butchers' shops." And on January 15: "There are no cabs because all the horses have been eaten."

After Paris had suffered more than four months of famine, France yielded to a humiliating defeat. By the terms of the armistice, signed January 28, 1871, France agreed to pay Prussia a billion-dollar indemnity and ceded the provinces of Alsace and Lorraine. Men of Paris, who saw themselves betrayed by their own government, rose in revolt in the name of the newly organized Commune. Street fighting broke out between Communards and government troops. Gustave Courbet served as Commune Councillor in Charge of Fine Arts from April 16 to May 11. On May 16 Communards destroyed the famous Vendôme Column, a Paris landmark, on the grounds that it was poor art.

Fighting raged for six weeks before the government troops could overpower the Communards. By May 29 their red flag had disappeared from Paris. In a series of merciless reprisals, the government executed hundreds of prisoners and deported others to the French island of New Caledonia. Gustave Courbet was accused of the destruction of the Vendôme Column and sentenced, on September 2, to six months in prison. In his cell he wangled paints and canvases and produced some of his finest work.

Mary Cassatt, missing all this tragedy and terror, was back safely in America with her family. She may have practiced her still-imperfect French on her mother. She probably went horseback riding with Alexander. He and Gardner, a rising young banker, were both on the road to success. That her brothers were going to be wealthy pleased Mary for one reason. Rich people could afford to buy paintings. They could hang in their homes great masterpieces such as one saw now only in the museums of Europe.

In Philadelphia she painted a full-length portrait of her two-year-old nephew, Edward Buchanan Cassatt, the first son of Alexander and his wife, Lois. His mother dressed him up for the occasion in a velvet suit with a lace collar. Mary's portrait was a good likeness, but showed neither the technical competence nor the striking use of color that characterized her later works.

She had brought back some paintings she had done in Paris, but none of her relations or friends in Philadelphia showed any enthusiasm for them. It was not that they judged them good or bad, but that, as they did not fail to remind her, after all the money her father had spent on her she still had not sold a single painting.

In the hope that she might find some less critical buyers in the newly rich West, she set out with a cousin for Chicago in the fall of 1871. They reached there just in time for the Great Chicago Fire. The fire wiped out most of the city, killed several hundred people, and destroyed some $200 million worth of property. Another loss was the early Mary Cassatt paintings, probably sent ahead. She and her cousin, the rest of their baggage intact, returned east.

Whatever Mary Cassatt's first distress, she had too much basic common sense to mourn long over the loss. The world was not going to miss much. She was still not the kind of painter she wanted to be. Since her French professors had failed to teach her what she wanted to know, perhaps she would do better to go directly to the "Old Masters" of Europe and study and copy their work.

With surprising ease, she persuaded her father to finance another trip abroad. She set sail almost immediately.

4

Rendezvous with the Old Masters

Rome, not Paris, was Mary Cassatt's first destination on her third European venture. Paris was still stricken with the aftereffects of the long siege and the insurrection that followed it. Mr. Cassatt would not have wanted his daughter to risk the privations and hardships that Parisians were suffering. Moreover, Mary had been dreaming of studying in Rome ever since her early teens.

What were her reactions to the "Eternal City," the fabulous Roman capital? Did she "bitterly detest it," as Nathaniel Hawthorne insisted he did a few years earlier when "Roman fever"—malaria—had taken his oldest daughter, Una? Was she appalled by the filth and the "noisome smell" of the narrow streets, which another American writer, William Dean Howells, would lament a few years later? Did the muddy waters of the Tiber depress her after the clear and sparkling Seine of Paris? Or, as is more likely, did her romantic spirit and her sense of history blind her to all but the beauty she had come to find?

Did she go sightseeing in the Catacombs of St. Sebastian, climb the flower-lined steps of the Piazza di Spagna, visit the Coliseum by moonlight, make a pilgrimage to the graves of Shelley and Keats with other tourists? Did she take a sip of the crystal waters of the Fountain of Trevi, thus making it certain, according to legend, that one day Rome would call her back?

Did she brave the Swiss Guard dressed up like "toy soldiers" in front of the Vatican Palace, make her way through the maze of galleries filled with the Vatican art treasures, stop to tie a black veil over her head to replace her bonnet so she would be permitted to enter the renowned Sistine Chapel and gaze upward at the incredible ceiling frescoes of Michelangelo showing God's creation of man?

Since she had come to meet the Old Masters, she cannot have neglected any of the numerous palaces, museums, and churches where Italy's masterpieces are found. She saw the works of some non-Italian artists as well and was considerably impressed with the portrait of Pope Innocent X by the seventeenth-century Spanish artist, Velásquez, who had done some of his best work in Italy.

Though Rome had much to offer an aspiring artist, she did not remain there. Instead she decided to go to the pic-

turesque town of Parma in north central Italy to do her
studying and copying. Her choice proved originality and
independence. In Rome there were almost as many American art students as in Paris. Munich and Antwerp were
also popular gathering places for American tourists and
students. Parma was off the beaten track.

The lure that Parma had for Mary Cassatt was the late
Renaissance painter Correggio. She may have become enamored of this artist at the Borghese Gallery in Rome,
where his painting of the mythological Greek princess,
"Danaë," hangs. Apparently she sensed that of all the Old
Masters she had seen thus far, including even the immortal Michelangelo and Leonardo da Vinci, Correggio could
teach her the things she most wanted to know. On learning that Parma was "full of Correggio," she hastened there.

In the Parma museum were his paintings "Madonna
and St. Jerome" and "Madonna Della Scodella." Correggio's frescoes adorned the monastery of St. Lodovico, the
church of San Giovanni Evangelista, and Parma's lovely
cathedral. The spirit of this artist seemed to hover in the
very air of Parma.

His religious subjects, like his mythological ones, were
painted in a fresh and joyous manner, totally missing in
the insipid imitations of the French Academicians. He
treated space as a "whirlpool of brightness," as one critic
described it; his incandescent background lighting was
spaced with the dazzling white of his clouds. In the fore-
shortening of his models, he showed a modern skill. According to one authority, Correggio marks "the dawn of a
beauty born of the soul of man." Mary Cassatt was most
enchanted with the luscious coloring of flesh and clothing
in his virgins and children and his lifelike and frolicsome
little angels.

While she was in Parma she discovered another Old

Master who delighted her—Parmigiano, so-called because Parma was his birthplace. His works were in an elongated style that foreshadowed El Greco, and Mary Cassatt later spoke of his "erect commanding figures." But it was Correggio who was her first great artistic love. From him she learned what kind of artist she wanted to become herself.

An Italian engraver and painter named Carlo Raimondi, who was a professor in the Parma Art Academy, became Mary's art instructor in Parma. He is thought to have introduced her to engraving techniques, though she was then interested only in painting. Fortunately he did not try to impose his own dry and conventional style on her. She made rapid progress under him and must have liked him better than her previous instructors. A portrait of a peasant woman she made at this time was dedicated, in French: "à mon ami [to my friend], C. Raimondo." She apparently spoke with him in French. She was not a linguist and never mastered more than a few essential phrases in Italian.

After all her floundering and uncertainty, Mary Cassatt was at last beginning to come into her own as an artist. In 1872 she did several canvases which, though painted in the Academic manner, showed vigor and spirit. One was "Hindu Dancing Girl" (The Bajadere). Another was "Bacchante," named after the female priestesses of the Greek god Bacchus. A third, which she did when she was back in Rome, was "During the Carnival" (Pendant le Carnaval), which pictures three people on a balcony in Seville. Somehow she got up the courage to ship it to Paris, as a submission to the Salon of 1872.

Unknowns submitting to the Salon were expected to give the names of their teachers. Mary listed "Soyer and Bellay," presumably two French artists she had studied with in Paris after she left Charles Chaplin. She signed

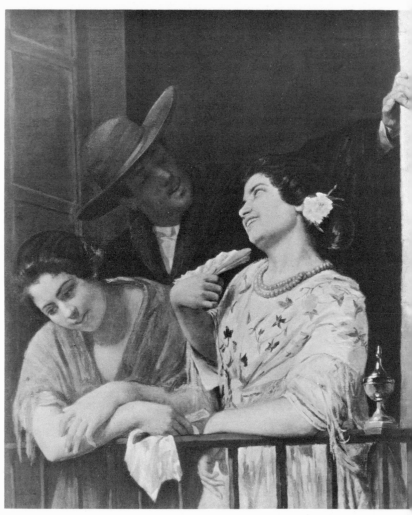

"During the Carnival" (Pendant le Carnaval), *Mary Cassatt. Philadelphia Museum of Art, Wilstach Collection.*

her entry "Mlle. Mary Stevenson." This rare use of her middle name may indicate either modesty or fear of bringing disgrace on the name of Cassatt.

The Salon accepted "Pendant le Carnaval." It was certainly a delirious moment when she learned the news. Now she could reassure her father that his money had not been wasted. Now her other relatives and her friends would have to admit that she was no amateur.

In this same year the Salon rejected Renoir's "Parisians Dressed in Algerian Costumes" (Parisiennes Costumées en Algérienne) and paintings of other artists far more advanced than she. Her own success may partly have been due to the fact that "Carnaval" did not offend the jury, that there was nothing very startling about it. No matter. Mary Cassatt took this triumph in her stride, just as she had accepted, without discouragement, her own exceedingly slow growth as an artist.

In her long years of apprenticeship, she had come to several conclusions. She still had much to learn. Before deciding on a style of her own, she must go on immersing herself in the works of more Old Masters and learning their techniques. As for art schools, most of them were too commercial. She had no desire to paint slick portraits for an easy sale.

In 1873 she went to Spain, where she did one of the best paintings of her early career—"Offrant le Panal au Torero"—which shows a young girl offering a sweet drink (known as a *panal*) to a bullfighter in a purple jacket, bright red cape, white shirt, and pink tie. The Salon accepted it in 1873. This time she signed herself boldly as "Stevenson-Cassatt (Mlle. Mary)."

Sisley, Monet, and Pissarro were too disgusted with the Salon to submit anything that year. Renoir had two canvases rejected. The Salon hung Édouard Manet's "Le Bon

Bock," a portrait of a stout bourgeois gentleman smoking his pipe and obviously relishing a glass of bock beer. Its human-interest appeal made it popular with the public, but Manet's young artist admirers were disappointed. They considered "Le Bon Bock" a letdown coming from the creator of "Déjeuner sur l'Herbe."

Mary used her same bullfighter model for another painting she did in Spain—"Toreador." In this one he wears a silver and blue jacket that contrasts strikingly with his red cape and tie. The composition was the best she had done to date. By any standards it was an excellent picture. That a young woman from Philadelphia should be able to capture on canvas the character of a Spanish bullfighter was in itself amazing. It has remained as one of the few successful portraits of male subjects she ever did.

She was living in Madrid and going almost daily to the Prado museum, a great red brick building whose poorly lit labyrinth of galleries housed many undistinguished paintings alongside some of the greatest art treasures of the world. Here Mary discovered the great Flemish painter Peter Paul Rubens, some of whose works had come into Spain's possession at the time of the Spanish conquest of Flanders. Rubens' bright, clear colors were soon reflected in her own canvases.

Overcome with a desire to see more works by Rubens, she took off for Antwerp, Belgium, where he had lived most of his life. She was copying one of his paintings in the Antwerp museum one day when she met a young Frenchman named Joseph Gabriel Tourny, who was also making Rubens copies. An indifferent artist, he earned his living by selling such copies. It was a casual encounter, but it had far-reaching results.

Mrs. Cassatt joined her daughter in Antwerp. Mary took the opportunity to do a fine portrait of her sympathetic and understanding mother in an elegant gown of black lace over cream-colored silk and a bonnet adorned with a red flower.

Soon afterward Mary Cassatt went to Haarlem, in Holland, to see the works of the Dutch painter Frans Hals, whom she also greatly esteemed. At the Haarlem museum she made a copy of his "Meeting of the Officers of the Cluveniers-Doelen," one of a series of commissioned portraits of civil guards in full regalia that Frans Hals had done with skill and realism. Mary was always proud of this copy and later would show it to young art students as proof of the benefits of studying and copying the Old Masters. That she chose this sedate commissioned group portrait rather than one of Hals' more lusty paintings of stout burghers and red-cheeked women, any of which would have been far easier to copy, reveals both her puritanical upbringing and her capacity for hard work.

Two years had passed since her arrival in Rome. In Italy, Spain, Belgium, and Holland, she had kept firmly to her resolution to seek knowledge and inspiration from the past. A yearning now stirred in her to return to the present.

In Paris, once more at peace and freed from the oppressive influence of Emperor Napoleon III, a cultural revolution was in the making. Following in the wake of the French Revolution a century before, the cultural revolution was a further step toward awarding the common people their place in the sun. The new heroes were neither the kings and queens nor the gods and goddesses so popular with the Academic artists. They were ordinary men and women, with dreams, passions, hopes, and frustrations familiar to all mankind.

It was a time when Émile Zola published *The Belly of Paris* (Le Ventre de Paris), in which the principal charac-

ters were the butchers and fishwives of the great Paris
market of Les Halles. It was a time when Edgar Degas was
using his great talent to sketch from life the scrawny little
gamines who made up the chorus of the ballet, and Camille Pissarro was trying his hand at painting lowly peasants at work in the fields. It was a time of ardent discussions on art, music, poetry, and the meaning of life; a time
of the growth of daily newspapers, and of a return to
nature, not as a romantic escape from the real world, but
as a vital part of it.

For certain artists, who were rebelling against the sterile standards of conservative art, this period marked the
fruition of their talents, the beginning of a golden decade.

There was no more stimulating place in the world than
Paris in the mid-1870's. Mary Cassatt returned there.

"Madame Cortier," Mary Cassatt. Courtesy of Maxwell Galleries, Ltd., San Francisco.

Degas had not submitted anything to the Salon that year. He was one of some thirty progressive artists who were weary of being at the mercy of the reactionary Salon jury and were boycotting it. They had decided to hold their own exhibition and thus bring their works directly to the public.

Among this group were Camille Pissarro and the three veterans of Gleyre's studio—Monet, Renoir, and Sisley. The oldest of the group was Eugène Boudin, now fifty-nine, who had first taught Monet to love landscape painting. Paul Cézanne, embittered by years of constant rebuffs, joined them only because of Pissarro. He adored Pissarro, who had been almost the first to recognize his talent. There was only one woman in the group, Berthe Morisot, now the sister-in-law of Édouard Manet. Manet himself would have nothing to do with their project and in fact felt that they were making a big mistake to defy the Salon.

Under the name of the Society of Artists, Painters, Sculptors, and Engravers, this group of thirty held its first exhibition from April 15 to May 15, 1874, in the studio of the photographer Nadar, on the Boulevard des Capucines. Admission was one franc, with fifty centimes more for a catalog, prepared by Renoir's brother, Edmond. The price was cheap enough to attract large numbers of visitors. Most of them had had their taste formed by the Salon. They did not know what to make of this new art.

Here were none of the giant canvases to which they were accustomed, showing imaginary scenes of an imaginary world in which all women were beautiful and all men noble and handsome. There were no battle scenes with heroic warriors, no castles or palaces, no nymphs, gods, or goddesses. There was nothing to transport them to a dream land where they could forget their own prosaic lives—as, in their opinion, art was supposed to do.

Edgar Degas, for example, had submitted a portrait of two slovenly laundresses at their ironing board. The excellence of the work went unnoticed and the only reaction was that his choice of subject was revolting. Such pitiful creatures were not worth a second glance, neither in real life nor on canvas.

Renoir's fine painting "La Loge," showing a middle-aged, well-dressed couple at the opera, also brought frowns of disapproval. There was nothing romantic or stirring about people going to the opera. The enchanting Paris street scenes of Pissarro were ignored because the setting was too familiar. As for the landscapes of Monet, they were simply dabs of color—as though, one wag commented, the artist had filled a pistol with paint and fired it at the canvas. Only the few who took the trouble to step back a few paces were aware that these dabs formed a lovely scene.

It is not known for sure whether Mary Cassatt attended the exhibition. Eager as she was to know what was going on, it would have been strange if she had missed it. If she was there, she would have noticed how the expressions of her fellow visitors changed from bewilderment to distaste, and then how, as if struck by the same contagion, they broke out in uproarious shrieks of mockery.

An American spectator summed up the general reaction when he reported the exhibition as "a laughable collection of absurdities."

The critics were even more caustic than the public. Paul Cézanne, who had submitted among other works his now-celebrated "The House of the Hanged Man" (La Maison du Pendu), received the most scathing comments.

"*Street Scene,*" *Camille Pissarro. Courtesy of the National Gallery, London.*

One critic called him "a kind of madman painting in the midst of delirium tremens."

The charming Berthe Morisot was treated with almost equal discourtesy. "This young lady is not concerned with trifling details," wrote Louis Leroy in the art review *Charivary*. "When she wants to indicate a hand she makes the same number of long brush strokes as there are fingers and the job is done."

Leroy's long and sarcastic article was filled with such deadly barbs, but unwittingly he gave a name to the group. Referring to an enticing Monet canvas titled "Impression, Sunrise" (Impression, Soleil Levant), he said: "I was sure of it. I had just been telling myself that as I was impressed there must be some impression in it."

This was the origin of the name "Impressionism." Applied first in derision, the term won serious acceptance. The 1874 exhibition, a landmark in art history, would later be referred to as the First Impressionist Exhibition.

What is meant by Impressionism exactly? It began when Monet, Renoir, Sisley, and Bazille went to the Forest of Fontainebleau to paint directly from nature. As it developed, under the leadership of Claude Monet, it became an ever more penetrating search for values and qualities in nature that escaped the casual observer. There was never a "school" of Impressionism. There is no glib definition. The Impressionist painters never took the time to devise theories about their style.

Impressionists were concerned with catching the transitory moods of nature, with the effects of light—on water, flowers, trees, fields of grain, or penetrating through mists, or breaking a spray into rainbow colors. They loved falling snow, swirling floods, smoke rising from a train, fogs that made solid buildings seem weightless. By preference they painted in the open air. From their point of view, artists who tried to paint nature in their studios, from sketches or memory or imagination, missed the subtle variations in coloring and atmosphere from hour to hour or moment to moment. Keenly observant, they detected that in nature shadows are neither black nor brown but a variety of shades, that colors merge into colors, that boundary lines, like perspective, are intellectual conceptions.

The dark colors of their predecessors became obsolete on their palettes. They preferred yellow, orange, crimson, violet, blue, and green. Rather than mixing colors, they applied pure colors to the canvas in dots and dashes.

Nor did they feel the need to go to the past, to mythology, to literature, or to the mysterious East for subject matter. All around them they saw beauty—in a suburban garden, a village street, a riverside café, a flower arrangement. When they could not afford models, they painted each other, their wives, their children, or the peasants that Pissarro did so well.

Their emphasis on the poetry of the humble, everyday things in life outraged the Academicians of the Salon perhaps even more than their nonconformist techniques. As they saw it, the Impressionists were as dangerous as social revolutionists.

Aside from Monet, Renoir, and Sisley, the only artists in the 1874 exhibition now classified as Impressionists were Pissarro and Berthe Morisot. Renoir would not remain an Impressionist. Pissarro and Berthe Morisot would experiment with other techniques. Only Monet and Sisley remained pure Impressionists to the end of their days.

Most of the thirty exhibitors even then objected to the Impressionist label. Edgar Degas, who almost never painted outdoors, rejected it vehemently. Nonetheless the Impressionists had a pervasive influence on his work, as

"Springtime," Claude Monet. Courtesy of the Walters Art
Gallery.

on the work of others—even Édouard Manet, who held himself apart from them, and Mary Cassatt, still in the glow of her first Salon successes.

Impressionists and non-Impressionists alike reeled under the disaster of that first independent exhibition in 1874. The blow was cruelest to those who depended on sales for their livelihood, like Pissarro and Monet, and like Alfred Sisley, whose English father had lost his money during the Franco-Prussian War. In the hope of recovering some of their losses, the group held an auction in March 1875, under the auspices of Paul Durand-Ruel. It, too, was a failure.

The visitors were so unruly and noisy that the auctioneer could not make himself heard. The paintings went for a pittance. Ten Renoirs sold for less than 100 francs ($20) each. Berthe Morisot fetched the best prices, an average of 250 francs.

Still, they made a few friends. The critic Théodore Duret decided he liked their works. An obscure government employee named Victor Choquet, who had by scrimping and saving bought up works of Delacroix, Daumier, and Corot, attended the auction quite by chance. On that date began his own remarkable collection of Renoirs, Monets, and Cézannes.

One thing could be said about the First Impressionist Exhibition and the auction that followed it. The artists were no longer obscure and unknown. Everyone was talking about them. If Mary Cassatt did not brave the rowdy crowds to attend either event, she certainly heard about them. Somewhere she saw the artists' paintings. Shortly she began recommending to American friends that they purchase not only Degas but Impressionist art.

The Salon of 1875 accepted a portrait of hers, titled "Mlle E. C.," but turned down another portrait, of her sister, Lydia, on the grounds that the colors were too bright. It was Mary's first setback in several years, and according to a letter she wrote a friend in Philadelphia, she was so discouraged that she could hardly work at all for the next three months. Nonetheless, she toned the colors down and submitted the picture again in 1876. It was accepted, along with a second canvas, "Portrait of Mme. W." She felt no sense of triumph. It still rankled deeply that against her better judgment she had been obliged to alter her sister's portrait. Never again did she submit a painting to the Salon.

Sometime in 1877 her Antwerp acquaintance, Joseph Tourny, brought Edgar Degas to meet her. She noted that the artist she had admired so long and reverently was not tall, although he had an arresting appearance. His complexion was swarthy. He had a small, dark beard and mocking eyes. His manners were flawless and he wore his expensive clothes with the air of someone accustomed to the best. Either Degas or Tourny explained the reason for their visit. Degas had come to invite her to exhibit with the Impressionists.

"I accepted with delight," she later told her first biographer, Achille Segard. "At last I could work in complete independence, without bothering about the eventual judgment of a jury. It was then I began to live."

The Impressionists had now held three exhibitions in all. The second and the third had attracted almost as many insults as the first. Some of their critics became more vitriolic each year. They were still the laughingstock of Paris, the outlaws of orthodox art circles. That she might be subjected to the same scorn and mockery if she joined their ranks does not seem to have worried Miss Mary Cassatt of Philadelphia. She had found what she wanted at last.

6

Edgar Degas

So far as is known, Mary Cassatt had never been in love
before she met Edgar Degas, nor had she betrayed a special interest in any young man. One reason certainly was
her all-consuming drive to be a good artist. Art meant
more than anything in the world to her, even marriage.
She enjoyed male companionship, always had more men
than women friends, but it is likely that she was bored by
the young men whom Philadelphia society deemed eligible, if indeed she did not scare them off by her forthright-

ness. As for foreigners, she may have shared the common American prejudice that they were all adventurers and not to be trusted. If so, that prejudice did not extend to include Edgar Degas.

How incredible that he had sought her out, almost as an equal, this artist she had admired so long! Her emotions were in a tumult after that first meeting. She could hardly have sorted them out or analyzed them. She was not by nature overly modest, especially about her work, but it made her feel actually humble that Degas recognized her as an artist. She could not expect this great genius to be interested in her as a woman. Yet he was.

About the time she met Degas, her family came to live with her in Paris. Mr. Cassatt, who had long since become reconciled to her odd choice of a profession, had retired from his brokerage house, Lloyd and Cassatt. With his savings and a small legacy from a relative, he reasoned he could live better abroad than in America and had accordingly brought Mrs. Cassatt and Lydia to Paris to join his artist daughter. They all took a sixth-floor apartment in Montmartre, near the Place Pigalle.

Though part of Paris, Montmartre had the air of a picturesque village. For years it had attracted artists. Pissarro and Sisley had painted its narrow cobblestone streets. In Montmartre was the Moulin de la Galette, an old mill converted into an outdoor café, which Renoir made immortal in his painting "Dancing at the Moulin de la Galette." In Montmartre also was the Café de la Nouvelle-Athènes, which had replaced the Café Guerbois as a meeting place for artists and writers. Two marble-topped tables were always reserved for Édouard Manet and his friends. Most of the Impressionists showed up there from time to time. Degas usually stopped by late in the evening. Another habitué was the Irish writer and amateur

"Dancing at the Moulin de la Galette," Auguste Renoir. Courtesy of the Louvre.

artist George Moore, who later reminisced about his evenings at the café. Through Degas, Mary Cassatt gradually met most of these people, but sitting around cafés was still off-bounds for a proper American woman.

With her family comfortably installed, she rented a studio near their apartment and set up a rigid work schedule for herself. While her father paid the expenses for their apartment and for their cook and other servants, he made it clear that she must take care of her studio expenses herself out of her earnings. Even with her Salon acceptances, this was not easy. Her sales were few, and since she was always striving for perfection, her production was not rapid. Each morning at eight she went to her studio and worked steadily, with a short break for the midday meal, until daylight failed.

After supper she turned to copper engraving, which she could do by the light of the lamp. She had taken up engraving as a form of discipline to improve her draftsmanship. Often she made engravings as a preliminary to paintings she had in mind. An engraving, lacking colors, reveals the strength or weakness of an artist. Through this enforced discipline Mary Cassatt developed strong and virile lines.

She was not alone in her fanatical dedication to work. In spite of the reputation critics had given the Impressionists of tossing their colors together at random, they all slaved as hard as bricklayers, stopping only when they ran out of canvases, paint, or paintbrushes. It was the same with Degas. A celebrated art critic once announced he was going to visit him at his studio. "If you wish," Degas said with a shrug, "but at the end of the day when it is dark." Daylight hours were too precious to waste in mere conversation, even for the sake of favorable reviews.

Yet in that period Degas always managed to find time

to see Mary Cassatt. He let her come to his studio and watch him at work. He came to her studio, too, to oversee what she was doing. He encouraged her with her engraving. They went to the Louvre and to various art exhibitions together. On occasion he came to dinner at the Cassatts' apartment. Mary's parents were charmed with this well-mannered, well-dressed, sophisticated and entertaining gentleman, so different from their preconceived notions of what artists were like. His very aristocratic snobbishness convinced them that he was a suitable companion for their daughter.

For one of her best paintings, "Little Girl in the Blue Armchair" (Le Salon Bleu), it is known that Degas not only advised her on the composition but actually did some of the work on it himself. He even supplied the model; the little girl was the daughter of one of his friends.

"Le Salon Bleu" shows the child, in white dress and plaid sash, sprawled out on a flower-patterned easy chair. A small dog sits in a similar chair opposite her. The design of the painting is formed by the irregular empty space of the floor and a third chair in the background. Mary submitted this work to the American section of the Paris Exposition of 1878 but it was turned down. She noted contemptuously that one of the three people composing the jury that rejected the painting was a pharmacist.

Mary also did a small self-portrait in 1878. Wearing a white dress with long sleeves and a high, full collar, and a flowered bonnet tied under her chin with a scarf, she is seated on a striped settee, leaning to the side and resting on one elbow. (The diagonal design her pose gives the composition is said definitely to show Degas' influence.) Her expression has a childlike wistfulness and is devoid of

"Little Girl in the Blue Armchair," Mary Cassatt. *National Gallery of Art, Washington, D.C., lent by Mr. and Mrs. Paul Mellon.*

"Self-Portrait," Mary Cassatt. Courtesy of Mrs. Richman Proskauer, New York.

coquetry. It is easy to see why the sophisticated Degas, accustomed to the feminine wiles of European women, was attracted to her.

No doubt her American accent amused him, but he liked the way she had of speaking her mind, plainly and bluntly. Her talent at painting amazed him, coming from a woman. He tended to regard women as inferior beings, but with Mary Cassatt he found an intellectual companionship, unique in his experience. He also found an avid listener. For while she was relatively well informed about art and not in the least hesitant to express her opinions, she did not pretend to know as much as he. In truth, she never forgot any of the advice he gave her, or any of his comments on artistic matters and artists he admired.

Their first conversations were certainly limited to the high level of art. As they knew each other better they talked about themselves. At one time or another Degas told her about his early life.

Born on July 19, 1834, he was descended from a noble French family who traced its ancestry back to the Crusades. Following the French Revolution, his grandfather, René-Hilaire de Gas, fell into disfavor with the anti-Royalists and fled to Italy to avoid arrest. There he started a small money-changing office, which in time became a bank. He prospered, married a woman from Genoa, and had ten children.

One of them was Pierre-Auguste-Hyacinth de Gas, who came to Paris to run a branch of his father's bank. He married a young woman named Celestine Musson, whose family had made a fortune in the West Indies from cotton, spices, sugar, and rum. They were the parents of Edgar, who changed his name from "de Gas" to "Degas" early in his twenties. He had two sisters and two brothers. One of them, René, ran the Musson family business in

New Orleans. Their mother died when Edgar was thirteen.

Edgar was still in his teens when his father took him to see a friend and art connoisseur, Monsieur Valpinçon, who owned "Odalisque au Turban" by Ingres. The painting made a deep impression on him. He studied law for a while, but at nineteen he was firmly resolved to be an artist himself. His father not only encouraged him but gave him a liberal allowance for his studies. Unlike Mary Cassatt, he matured rapidly as an artist.

A self-portrait made when he was twenty shows him romantic and handsome in appearance but with an air of disillusionment that seems to indicate he had already left his youth behind him. The next year he went to Naples to visit the Italian branch of his family. His girl cousins were captivated, but he was immune to feminine charms. He left them to go to Florence, where he copied Raphael, Botticelli, and other Italian masters, besides making some charming sketches of street scenes, children playing, and beautiful Florentine women in long skirts.

At the time of the Paris World's Fair of 1855—which both he and little Mary Cassatt attended—he met Ingres for the first time. "Draw lines, young man," the old French master advised him, as he had so many hopeful artists. Degas paid more heed to his advice than any other. In this case the disciple would surpass the master.

He made more trips to Italy in the next several years. "Poetry breathes from everything here," he wrote of that country. In 1857 he did a superb portrait of a Roman beggar woman, "Mendiante Romaine." It was the first thing he had done in which he took pride, but he was not satisfied then or ever.

He tried his hand at everything. Only his military service in the Franco-Prussian War took him away from his

"Self-Portrait," Edgar Degas. *The Metropolitan Museum of Art, bequest of Stephen C. Clark, 1960.*

work for any length of time. He did paintings, pastels, sketches, and engravings. His portrait of his Italian relatives, "The Bellelli Family" (La Famille Bellelli) was remarkable for its realism and informal posing. He did several large paintings on the classical themes so popular with the Salon jury, to show they could be treated in a fresh and exciting manner. One was "Young Spartan Girls Provoking Some Boys" (Petites Filles Spartiates Provoquant des Garçons), in which the youthful models look like Paris street urchins. In this early period of his career he also did some brilliant works of horses and horse racing. He painted young ballet dancers, not only in full costume under the glamour of spotlights, but working at the bar, or sitting on benches in the awkward poses of adolescents. For a change he turned to the laundresses who were to outrage visitors to the First Impressionist Exhibition. He liked doing circus performers and orchestra musicians.

Only landscapes had little appeal for him. Sedentary by nature, he preferred the solitude and comfort of his studio to the out of doors. Already, when Mary Cassatt met him, he had the reputation of being a recluse.

When friends asked him why he did not get married, he said, with some degree of seriousness, that he was obsessed by the fear that one day his wife would say, "Now that's a pretty picture you painted." That was certainly one remark Mary Cassatt was never guilty of making to him.

Her own fear at this stage of her career was that she might be forced to paint "potboilers." She could not bear the thought of lowering her standards for money. In October 1878 Mr. Cassatt wrote Alexander that "Mame" was in good spirits, that a French collector had bought one picture and ordered another. But two months later he confessed to his son that although she had been working diligently she had sold nothing lately.

She shipped a batch of paintings to a Philadelphia art dealer named Herman Teubner, recommended by a friend, Mrs. Mitchell, but Teubner was apparently neither active at selling pictures nor good at answering letters. At one time he had fifteen unsold Cassatt paintings. When the artist sent word that she would accept $700 for the lot, he did not reply. "A scamp," Mr. Cassatt called him.

Mary Cassatt finally decided that not Teubner but Philadelphia was at fault. ("A prophet is not without honour, etcetera," wrote Mr. Cassatt to Alexander.) New York was now replacing Philadelphia as America's cultural center. She arranged to send some pictures to a dealer there. Though her success was not spectacular, one way or another, she managed to avoid "potboilers."

Her problems were slight compared to those of the Impressionists, after the successive failures of their first three exhibitions. "Profound desolation reigns in the Impressionist camp," Paul Cézanne wrote his childhood friend, the novelist Émile Zola. "Gold is not exactly flowing into their pockets and pictures are rotting on the spot."

Pissarro, whose wife was expecting a fourth child, owed money to the butcher, the baker, and almost everyone else. Renoir, who survived by accepting portrait commissions from bourgeois clients, was so disgusted with the result of the Impressionists' exhibitions that in 1878 he broke the agreement they had made to boycott the Salon.

Monet was in the most desperate straits of all. His wife, Camille, fell seriously ill after giving birth to their second son, but he could not afford a doctor for her. Their cottage was bare of food and furniture. He had run out of paints. At this critical moment, his friend Gustave Caillebotte came to the rescue. Caillebotte was a well-to-do ma-

rine engineer whom Monet had met at Argenteuil-sur-
Seine. Caillebotte had helped him build a boat that
served as a studio. He had considerable artistic talent and
under Monet's influence became a very good Impressionist himself.

Caillebotte's loyalty and Degas' continued support
played a large role in the opening of a fourth exhibition
in 1879, two years after the last. Renoir, Sisley, and
Cézanne did not exhibit, nor did Berthe Morisot, who
was pregnant. Monet refused to leave his sick wife to come
to Paris, but Caillebotte collected some of his canvases to
show, including several he had purchased.

There were several newcomers in the exhibition. One
was Paul Gauguin, a prosperous stockbroker and a Sunday
painter, brought in by Camille Pissarro. Another was
Mary Cassatt. It was two years now since Degas had first
asked her to join them, and she had lost none of her original enthusiasm. She was the only American to exhibit and
the only woman except for Madame Braquemond, the
wife of the engraver Félix Braquemond.

Her contribution was a painting called "La Loge." It
shows a young woman in a pink evening dress, with au-
burn hair and glowing skin, seated in an opera box holding a fan, against a background of red hangings and the
curved tier of other boxes. The rich coloring suggests Renoir; the model's dynamic pose signals the Degas influence. But the portrait is in Mary Cassatt's own style, at its
best, as it finally had emerged.

The exhibition opened April 10, 1879. By five o'clock
that afternoon, the receipts were more than 400 francs.
"We are saved," Caillebotte wrote Monet, a little prematurely. In spite of the many visitors, Paris art critics were
just as unpleasant as ever about nearly all the exhibitors
except for Degas and the American, Mary Cassatt.

One of the more moderate critics, who did not allow his prejudice against Impressionism to affect his judgment of all the exhibitors, was Georges Lafenestre, who wrote in the *Revue des Deux Mondes:*

> M. Degas and Mlle. Cassatt are, nevertheless, the only artists who distinguish themselves in the group of independents and who offer some attraction and some excuse in the pretentious show of window dressing and infantile daubing in the midst of which one is almost surprised to find their neglected canvases. Both have a lively sense of luminous arrangements in Parisian interiors; both show unusual distinction in rendering the flesh tints of women fatigued by late nights and the shimmering light of fashionable gowns. . . . M. Degas is more mature and able and is a more experienced draughtsman.

That Degas received the higher praise seemed quite natural to Mary, who was dazzled at even being mentioned with him. Mr. Cassatt jubilantly wrote Alexander that every leading daily French paper mentioned the exhibition and nearly all of them praised "Mame." To be sure, the one American paper in Paris that had a review spoke of her rather disparagingly, but one could expect no better. He had a low opinion of the American colony in Paris and kept clear of them, he claimed, to avoid being "mixed in their gossip."

At the close of the exhibition on May 11, there were 6,000 francs in the treasury, excluding expenses. They were divided equally among the exhibitors, 439 francs for each one. Mary Cassatt used her share to buy a Degas and a Monet.

About her own really spectacular success, she shrugged her shoulders. "Too much pudding!" she said.

"Mary Cassatt at the Louvre" (*Au Louvre: La Peinture*), Edgar Degas. S. P. Avery Collection, Prints Division, The New York Public Library, Astor, Lenox, and Tilden Foundations.

She and Degas saw more of each other than ever in the next year. Their trips to the Louvre inspired him to use her as a model in two prints. The first was an etching and aquatint, "Au Louvre: Musée des Antiques," in which she stands with her back to the spectator, resting on a closed umbrella and looking at a sixth-century Etruscan tomb. Close by, a woman sits holding a catalog. It is probably Mary's sister, Lydia. The second print, an etching, "Au Louvre: La Peinture," is very similar, except that Mary is seen through a doorway leading into a picture gallery. Both show her slender, elegant figure in a narrow-waisted tailored suit, and her extravagantly feminine hat. The prints somehow reflect the esteem and slightly amused affection with which Degas regarded his friend from Philadelphia.

He gave more definite proof of that esteem toward the end of 1879, when he asked her help on a pet project of his. This was an art review to be called *Day and Night* (Le Jour et La Nuit), which would reproduce regularly engravings done by the Impressionists, or "Independents," as Degas preferred to call their group. Ernest May, a banking friend, and Monet's friend Gustave Caillebotte had agreed to finance the publication.

For the first issue Degas planned to contribute one of his etchings of Mary Cassatt at the Louvre. She did a soft-ground etching and aquatint for it, called "In the Opera Box," similar to her painting "La Loge." Both of them worked, literally day and night, to get that first issue ready to go to press.

During this period they were closer together than at any other time before or after. To work intimately with a man of Degas' genius and integrity may well have been the most thrilling experience of Mary's life. There has been a good deal of speculation as to whether they were in

love, whether they were lovers at this time. There are in-
dications that they were, but no one will ever know for
sure. They were both discreet by nature and said nothing
to feed the rumors that floated around them.

Later, apparently by mutual consent, they destroyed
each other's letters. For art scholars this is a regrettable
loss, for it would be fascinating to read the correspondence between this worldly and cultured French artist
and Mary Cassatt of Philadelphia, who was still naive in
many ways and whose acquired culture was mostly self-
taught. Doubtless Degas gave her a great deal of advice
about her art career; he was generous in this respect not
only with her but with all his friends. Mary certainly con-
sulted him on many matters, but being neither docile nor
meek, she must have stood up to him firmly when she dis-
agreed. Whether there were any tender passages in their
letters will remain a mystery.

For some reason never clearly explained, not even the
first issue of *Le Jour et La Nuit* appeared. Mr. Cassatt took
its collapse as evidence that not even such socially accepta-
ble artists as Monsieur Degas could be depended on. To
Alexander he wrote that Degas was never ready for anything, and that this time he had thrown away an excellent
chance for all his fellow artists.

In addition to her futile labors on *Le Jour et La Nuit,*
Mary was busy that winter and spring preparing for the
Fifth Impressionist Exhibition, as future art historians
would call it. (At the time, on Degas' insistence, it was announced as the Exhibition of Independents.)

In advance, posters in bright red against a green background were prepared to announce the event. Degas did
not think it fitting to put the names of the exhibitors on
the posters, but Gustave Caillebotte overruled him. He
had a paternal feeling for his fellow artists and wanted

them to get all the publicity they could. Mary still refused to let her name be used, probably thinking it unladylike. In this she was joined by Berthe Morisot, Édouard Manet's sister-in-law and mother of a lovely baby daughter named Julie.

This 1880 exhibition had only eighteen participating artists, and of these Caillebotte, Berthe Morisot, Pissarro, and Armand Guillaumin were the only Impressionists. Besides Renoir and Sisley, Claude Monet, their leader from the beginning, was missing. Camille, his wife, had died of tuberculosis the summer before, leaving him with two small sons. Near-starvation had led to her illness. Poverty had prevented proper medical care. Monet could not forgive himself. He had been the most uncompromising of them all. Even in their most desperate times he had refused to accept portrait commissions, decorate cafés with murals, or do other commercial jobs. Camille, of whom his family disapproved, had stood by him loyally. He blamed himself for her death. When success came later, it was meaningless to him.

Mary Cassatt knew Monet only slightly. Unlike Degas, he did not discourse on the Italian masters. He had little formal education. Once, in an acid mood, she dismissed him as "stupid." Nor did she care much for Renoir, whose earthy humor perhaps offended her sense of propriety. Though she held herself socially aloof, she admired them both as artists, bought their paintings, and urged others to do so.

She submitted at least two paintings of her own to the fifth exhibition. One of them showed a young woman in yellow sitting in an opera box—the same theme as her previous success, "La Loge." The other portrayed two society matrons drinking tea, for which Lydia served as one of the models. These two paintings are indicative of Mary

"The Cup of Tea," Mary Cassatt. *The Metropolitan Museum of Art, gift of an anonymous donor, 1922.*

Cassatt's limited subject matter. Unlike Degas, she rarely went outside her social class in search of new faces and movement patterns. Over and over she painted the sort of women she met socially, but she did so with great variety in color and composition and with increasing mastery.

She also displayed several prints at the exhibition, but the catalog was incomplete and did not list them. On Degas' advice, they were strikingly mounted on yellow paper with purple frames.

Émile Zola attended the exhibition and noticed her work for the first time. "Mademoiselle Cassatt, an American, I believe, recently made her debut with some remarkable works of unusual originality," he wrote in the review *Voltaire*. But the French art critics were less lavish in their praise than before, and the American papers published in Paris again ignored her, almost pointedly, it seemed.

But the following year, at the Sixth Impressionist Exhibition that opened in April 1881, she had her greatest triumph to date. She submitted three paintings she had done while on vacation with her family at Marly the previous summer. One, "The Cup of Tea," showing a woman in an elaborate pink gown drinking tea, had the theme she did so well and so often. Another was of Lydia knitting in the Cassatts' garden. The third, and most interesting, showed her mother reading to her grandchildren Katherine, Robert, and Elsie (Alexander's three youngest children). Edgar Degas saw these paintings in advance of the exhibition and commented that they were "much more firm and noble" than anything she had done before. Critics confirmed his judgment. Even the sarcastic Albert Wolff of the Paris newspaper *Figaro,* who lashed into the Impressionists year after year, had pleasant things to say of Mary Cassatt.

The novelist and critic J. K. Huysmans was positively ecstatic about her. The year before he had claimed that her work was derived from Degas and certain English masters, but now he called her "an artist who owes nothing any longer to anyone, an artist wholly impressive and personal." He described "The Cup of Tea" as having "a fine sense of Parisian elegance." In her portraits of children, interiors, and gardens, "so much cherished by the English," she had found the way to escape from sentimentality. Thanks to Miss Cassatt, he had seen "ravishing youngsters, quiet bourgeois scenes painted with a delicate and charming tenderness." Mary Cassatt, he concluded, "achieves something that none of our painters could express, the happy contentment, the quiet friendliness of an interior."

Huysman's praise for the way she did her nieces and nephew may have confirmed something she had only over the past year been sensing—that she had a special affinity for portraying children.

Only one of the three American papers in Paris mentioned her, but among the French, at least, she was now fully established. Other artists of note and persons prominent in the art world sought her acquaintance. As a result of the exhibition she also made a number of sales.

Degas fared less well at the hands of the critics. He exhibited a wax statuette that he had been trying to perfect for the past twelve years, "Little Dancer, Aged Fourteen" (Petite Danseuse de Quatorze Ans). Albert Wolff of *Figaro* dismissed this impudent little dancer in a tattered ballet dress as "an interesting experiment" and called Degas the "God of Failures." Happily Degas could not have cared less what Wolff or any other critic said of him. In fact, the "Petite Danseuse" established Degas as a first-rate sculptor. In bronze, she is now in the Louvre.

After the exhibition Émile Zola, who had previously supported the group, commented sourly that Impressionism had ceased to exist. Yet on the whole the exhibitors received more favorable notices than in any of their previous showings.

The Paris winter of 1881 was so foggy and gloomy that there were days when Mary could not see to work. Then she took off to her milliner to buy a new hat. Degas frequently went with her. He was intrigued by the little milliner's apprentices with "their rough red hands" and did many sketches of them. He also used Mary Cassatt as a model for a painting, "At the Milliner's" (Chez la Modiste), which shows her trying on a hat in a complicated pose that would have been difficult for a regular model.

Neither she nor Degas participated in the Seventh Impressionist Exhibition in 1882. The dealer Paul Durand-Ruel sponsored it and paid for the space, but insisted only Impressionists should exhibit. He did not use the term so strictly as to exclude Degas and Mary Cassatt but did eliminate some of Degas' other friends. Degas withdrew in protest and Mary followed his example, as she always did in this period of her life.

Mr. Cassatt took a sly pleasure in this disagreement between artists, as proof of his suspicion that artists were less stable than bankers and brokers. Berthe Morisot, who liked both Mary Cassatt and Degas, was deeply distressed.

They missed a splendid showing of the finest works of Monet, Sisley, Pissarro, Berthe Morisot, Paul Gauguin, and Renoir. One of Renoir's submissions was his now well-known "The Luncheon of the Boating Party" (Déjeuner des Canotiers), which portrays a luncheon at an outdoor restaurant on an island in the Seine; one of the pretty models was his future wife. The exhibition brought many enthusiastic press notices and only a few bad ones,

"At the Milliner's," Edgar Degas. The Metropolitan Museum of Art, H. O. Havemeyer Collection, bequest of Mrs. H. O. Havemeyer, 1929.

but it would be four years before there would be another one.

It must have been a letdown for Mary Cassatt not to have the annual exhibitions to look forward to. In May 1883 her father wrote Alexander that "Mame" was having one of her gloomy spells, which he explained by saying that all artists suffered from them. A few weeks later he wrote that she was not at all well; he thought she was "dyspeptic."

Her depression and her illness may have had something to do with Degas. She had known him for six years now. The romantic phase of their relationship, which reached its height while they were working on *Le Jour et La Nuit,* had passed. While her esteem for him as an artist never faltered, she was discovering that he was a most temperamental person, and could be cruel and cutting. About this time she sent some American friends to his studio. Since she had praised his works, they wanted to buy something from him. Later they repeated a sarcastic remark he had made about her. It seemed a mean return for the favor she had tried to do him. Indignant, furious—and probably brokenhearted—she refused to see him for a long time.

By 1884 they were reconciled, for Degas did a portrait of her that year. It was not very flattering and made her look considerably older than her own self-portrait done six years before. Much later she asked Durand-Ruel to sell it "quietly," so that no one would know she had posed for it. He succeeded so well that no one knew its whereabouts until 1951, when the Wildenstein Gallery acquired it from a Tokyo collection. Subsequently it was sold to a New York art collector named André Meyer, under its proper title, "Portrait of Mary Cassatt."

7

An American Family in France

Beginning with the arrival of her family in Paris, Mary Cassatt had two lives. One had to do with her artistic career, her French artist friends, and Degas. It had a distinctly French flavor. The other, encompassing her relationship with her relatives and friends from home, although set in France, was wholly American. Though these two lives inevitably overlapped at times, it was surprising to what extent Mary Cassatt kept them in separate channels.

That she was pleased to have her family with her, there is no doubt. Still there were certain disadvantages. Neither her parents nor Lydia were in good health. She felt responsible for their welfare. On her shoulders fell the burden of deciding where they should live, where they should take their vacations. Nor could she travel herself when the notion struck her, as she had in the past. But if she ever felt any resentment at being tied down, she kept it to herself. In her relatively few letters to America in this period, she often spoke of her parents' health but rarely mentioned her career, her work, or her French friends.

As for Mr. Cassatt, he settled down with zest to being a retired American in Paris. In his own fashion, he loved Paris better than any other city. An ardent pedestrian, he spent his days exploring its seemingly inexhaustible monuments and historical sites. To his oldest grandson, Eddie, he wrote that Paris offered "a thousand and one delights" —goat carriages, the Guignol Theater, and on Sunday evenings fireworks "finer than any you can see in America." He was less happy outside of Paris.

In the summer following the Fourth Impressionist Exhibition of 1879, the first in which Mary Cassatt participated, she and her father took a trip to the Isle of Wight in the English Channel, which they followed with a tour through Switzerland into the mountains of northern Italy. Both journeys were lavish in scenic beauty, but Mary did not enjoy herself as much as she might have if she had been on her own. Mr. Cassatt was a white-haired, white-bearded old man now. Age had made him demanding and crotchety, especially when faced with the inconveniences of travel.

Mrs. Cassatt met them both at Lausanne, in Switzerland. She was shocked at how pale and exhausted her daughter looked and took her to Divonne on the Swiss border for a rest. Mary kept worrying because she had been unable to work for three months and still had to get ready for the 1880 exhibition. She did not really feel like herself again until she got back to her studio in Paris.

In America, Alexander was doing better and better. Early in 1880 he was promoted from third vice-president in charge of transportation for the Pennsylvania Railroad Company to first vice-president. His father praised him for his financial success but cautioned him not to waste his money. "Most anybody, they say, can make money," he wrote. "Only the wise know how to keep it."

In view of the enormous fortune that Alexander Cassatt would later accumulate, there is something touching, and a little droll, in his father's pleas for frugality. In any case he was always a dutiful son. One of the first results of his new prosperity was a trust fund he set up for his parents. This made it possible for them to purchase their own carriage and pony. Previously they had depended on hired cabs for transportation, which Mr. Cassatt considered "anything but pleasant and hardly safe," all the more since the hack horses were usually "miserable brutes." Mrs. Cassatt, who had a heart condition, could now ride in much greater comfort. Mary had always loved horses and was delighted to have a pony that she could make sure was not mistreated.

Following the 1880 exhibition, she rented a villa at Marly, near Versailles, for her family's summer vacation. For art lovers, Marly will always recall Alfred Sisley's lovely paintings of "The Floods of Port Marly." Since it was not far from Paris, the Cassatts avoided the fatigue of traveling. They could settle down and relax in their own place. Moreover, Mary could paint. From then on she avoided any lengthy tours with her father.

"*Mother and Child*," *Mary Cassatt. The Metropolitan Museum of Art, H. O. Havemeyer Collection, bequest of Mrs. H. O. Havemeyer, 1929.*

The Alexander Cassatts also came to Europe that summer, with their four children—Eddie, Robert, Elsie, and Katherine. It was the first lengthy vacation Alexander had taken since he started working for the Pennsylvania Railroad. He and Lois stayed mostly in Paris and London, leaving their children with their nursemaid in Marly.

It had been a long time since Mary Cassatt had been around children. She talked to them as though they were adults. To her delight, little Robert showed signs of artistic talent. She encouraged him every way she could.

She and the children made numerous excursions in the Cassatt carriage. At Versailles they visited the charming Petit Trianon and saw the exquisite suite of rooms in which Queen Marie Antoinette had once lived. Another day they went to a public garden, where Elsie rode in a miniature carriage drawn by an ostrich and Katherine mounted an elephant. They watched a balloon ascension, which the children regarded with fascination mingled with terror.

Late in the summer, when their parents came to Marly, they found that all the children were deeply attached to their "Aunt Mame." In a letter to her sister, Lois Cassatt lamented that "strange to say," they seemed to prefer Mary to the other members of the family.

Alexander's hope that his wife would share his affection for Mary had never been realized. Perhaps he had tried too hard. In the same letter to her sister, Lois confided that she found something "utterly obnoxious" about "that girl," adding that Mary was self-important and "never criticized any human being in any but the most disagreeable way."

It is easy to understand why Lois felt uncomfortable around her sister-in-law. Her outlook on life was provincial. Affluence had not made her more tolerant of the opera and the theater. The simple working people and peasants, whom Renoir, Monet, and especially Pissarro found so congenial, had more respect for art than she. Her interests were limited to home and family, and to clothes and the other outward trappings of wealth.

In contrast, Mary Cassatt was an emancipated woman at a time when emancipated women were rare. Not only was she well versed in the field of art, but she had read widely, if rather haphazardly, and could discuss literature and politics with anyone. That she was sure of herself in many subjects utterly foreign to her sister-in-law was enough in itself to make Lois feel she was "obnoxious." She was probably right, however, in detecting a touch of vinegar in Mary's nature.

Mary seemed to have remained utterly oblivious to Lois' dislike. Probably for that reason there never was an open break. But the difference between them was too vast for any intimate friendship.

At Marly that summer, Mary gave Alexander the first of many lectures on the wisdom of investing some of his money in French paintings, particularly those of Edgar Degas. He listened but did not react at once. She also undertook to paint his portrait. The results did not satisfy her. She could not get him to relax. Moreover, his dark business suit did not lend itself to decorative designs, as did the colorful clothes of her feminine models.

She was much more pleased with her group portrait of Mrs. Cassatt reading to her grandchildren Katherine, Robert, and Elsie. This was the portrait that would be such a sensation at the Sixth Impressionist Exhibition.

On his return to America, Alexander shipped his family a large Christmas package, with apples, sweet potatoes, hams, canvasback ducks, and other strictly American produce. Mary Cassatt was thrilled to have "real American apples" and told her mother she resented every one they gave away. Mrs. Cassatt said tartly she was glad there was something American Mary liked better than the French equivalent. Her daughter retorted that she had never denied living was far better at home, though the French certainly made the best of what they had. Obviously she had not yet succumbed to the world-famous French cuisine.

Following the 1881 exhibition, she purchased a Pissarro and a Monet for Alexander, at a cost of 800 francs (about $160) for both. She tried to get him a Degas, but that artist was not in the mood to sell. With these two paintings, Alexander Cassatt became the second person in America to own Impressionist art. The first was Louisine Elder, who had followed the purchase of her first Degas with a Monet and a Pissarro, also on Mary's advice.

Not even the stocks and bonds that Alexander Cassatt undoubtedly held would undergo anything like the astronomical increase in value of the paintings his sister practically forced on him. Years later Impressionist paintings would become the rage in American museums and among private collectors, but it was Mary Cassatt who started the trend.

In the summer of 1881 she took her family to a villa at Louveciennes, where Pissarro had once lived and painted and which was not far from Marly. Every day she rode horseback on an old racer, "gentle as a lamb with plenty of spirit." Gardner, her banker brother, joined them. It was the first time he had been abroad since they were children.

She did not work too hard that summer, though one of her most popular pictures dates from approximately this period. This was "Woman and Child Driving," a careful composition showing a woman sitting in a carriage holding the reins, a little girl with long golden curls beside

"Woman and Child Driving," Mary Cassatt. Philadelphia Museum of Art, Wilstach Collection.

her, and a groom in the rear, facing backward. Mary's favorite pony, Bichette, is pulling the carriage, though only his tail and back are visible.

She did another painting of Bichette with Lydia feeding her oats. Mary's gentle older sister had been her most obliging model ever since she came to Paris, but her health was failing. Their doctor would diagnose her ailment as Bright's disease. Modeling became increasingly difficult. Mary's last portrait of her was "Woman Making Tapestry" (Femme à la Tapisserie). In the winter of 1881 Mrs. Cassatt took Lydia to southern France in the vain hope that the warm climate would be good for her. They all went to Louveciennes again the next summer. With Lydia ill, Mary hired a model to come to the villa every day.

That fall was a rapid sequence of upheavals for them. In October, Gardner, the confirmed bachelor of the family, married a girl from Virginia named Jennie Carter. Less than a month after his marriage came the tragedy of Lydia's death. Later in November Alexander and his family arrived in Paris with the announcement that he had resigned as first vice-president of the Pennsylvania Railroad. At forty-two he had decided to spend the rest of his life in leisure and travel.

His resignation caused considerable comment in railroad circles. It was hinted that he was piqued because a less capable man had been given the post of president of the Pennsylvania Railroad. The official story was that he was going to devote himself to breeding thoroughbred horses. At any rate, Alexander had enough money to live more than comfortably.

Eddie, his oldest son, enrolled in the French military school École Monge. Mary did a series of aquatints and drypoints of the three younger children, Robert, Katherine, and Elsie. To keep them amused while she sketched, she told them stories and supplied them with toys and books that she kept in her studio. She also tried her hand at another portrait of Alexander, but it was even less successful than the one she had done at Marly.

Much of her social life that winter revolved around her brother's family. They went to the theater to see Sarah Bernhardt, whom Lois said she "hated." It was a concession on her part to go to the theater at all. Several times Mary went horseback riding with Alexander in the Bois de Boulogne. She escorted the little girls to dancing school, and one day took them and Lois to see the spectacular panorama of a battle scene in the Franco-Prussian War, by the French painter Detaille. Another time they attended the opening of an exhibition of young artists, held in the galleries of Georges Petit, a dealer who was beginning to encroach on Durand-Ruel. She also took her brother and sister-in-law to visit the studio of "Mr. Degas," as Lois called the artist.

The two Cassatt families celebrated Christmas of 1882 together, at the apartment of Mary and her parents. Alexander had lavish gifts for everyone. Their far less affluent host and hostesses were not to be outdone. In addition to dolls and toys for the children, they gave Lois a beautiful lace scarf and a ring made up of five gold bands set with nine small diamonds. This, with all their other hospitality, seems to have toned down Lois' resentment against her sister-in-law.

The Alexander Cassatts left for London in April 1883. James Whistler, now a well-known portrait painter, had taken up residence there. Alexander engaged him to do a portrait of Lois in a riding costume. Mary Cassatt went to London later that year and called on Whistler to see how he was getting along with it. She saw enough to convince her it was a "Work of Art" and quoted "young John Sargent" as saying, "It is a good thing to have a portrait by Whistler in the family." But year after year passed and still Whistler did not complete the portrait, giving one excuse after another. Mary Cassatt became so annoyed with him, she would never again say anything good about her fellow American expatriate artist.

After Alexander and Lois went back to America, she took it on herself to keep an eye on her nephew Eddie, who was not very happy at the École Monge. The two of them went to Passy to see the greenhouses; to Bougival, where her horse Deauville was recuperating from an operation for lameness; and to the races of the Grand Prix, from which they returned "as white with dust as millers."

Eddie fell sick in July, and Mary took him to a hotel at Fontainebleau to recover. He wrote his mother all about their stay. Luckily they had not brought Batty, Aunt Mary's dog, he said. He would have had to carry him in addition to her valise, shawl strap, and two umbrellas, all while getting train tickets and finding a compartment on the train with space enough to hold all their things.

At the hotel there was "a whole gang" of Cook's tourists, who made an awful racket. Every tenth man they saw was a soldier. Aunt Mary was busy on a watercolor of Eddie, just one foot square. One day they took a lovely drive, climbed a mountain, and went into an "old brigand's cavern," which had a dining room, a chimney, and a dark passage. Their coachman had caught a baby squirrel. All in all, Eddie assured his mother, he was having a "snap time."

Later in July, Gardner Cassatt brought his young bride, Jennie, to Paris. They all attended Eddie's graduation from the École Monge. After they had seen him off for America, Mary and her mother joined the Gardner Cassatts on the Isle of Wight. Jennie wrote home that their hotel was frightfully expensive and "abominable," but that they enjoyed seeing the "Lords and Ladies" who vacationed on the island. Mary was, as usual, seasick on both Channel crossings.

She was still intent on making Alexander an art collector, and in 1883 she bought him four more Monet landscapes, another Pissarro, Berthe Morisot's "River Scene," Manet's "View in Holland," and Degas' "Ballet Class," in addition to two Renoir figure sketches. She tried to interest him in some Renoir paintings, but both he and Lois were immune to the charm of that artist. In fact, Alexander passed up most of her recommendations, partly because Lois objected to his throwing money away on "rubbish," her term for modern art.

Besides her chronic heart trouble, Mrs. Cassatt had been suffering from rheumatism. In December Mary took her to warm and sunny Spain. It was not much of a vacation for Mary, who spent most of her time in dreary hotel rooms, looking after her sick mother and waiting for the arrival of tardy Spanish doctors. Mrs. Cassatt seemed to be improving, but when they went to Madrid to "do" the huge Prado, she suffered a relapse. They came back to Biarritz, on the French Atlantic coast. Mary spent the next months commuting back and forth to Paris, where she was looking for a new apartment. The five flights of stairs they had to climb to reach their Montmartre apartment were too great a strain for her mother, though Mr. Cassatt, who detested moving, would not admit it.

Over his protests, Mary Cassatt rented a high-ceilinged and spacious apartment at 14, rue Pierre Charron, in the fashionable Paris area near the Trocadero. They paid the equivalent of $65 a month. She took one of the large rooms for her studio. The first painting she hung was a

"Alexander Cassatt and His Son, Robert Kelso Cassatt,"
Mary Cassatt. Philadelphia Museum of Art, Wilstach Collec-
tion.

small canvas showing a girl's head, done by her nephew Robert. Her hope that he would one day become an artist was revived when Degas commented he could not believe it was done without help. Robert never did fulfill her dream for him, but later became a banker, like his Uncle Gardner.

Robert and Alexander came to Paris late in 1884, with Alexander's manservant Louis, who always looked after him. Mary took Robert to see Bartholdi's bronze Statue of Liberty, which two years later would grace New York Harbor. Robert described it, not very poetically, as "an immense affair."

During their stay, Mary did a portrait of Alexander seated in an armchair, and Robert on the arm of the chair. According to Mrs. Cassatt, Robert "wriggled about like a flea" and "teased his poor Aunt" during the sittings, but Alexander was completely relaxed. It was the best portrait she ever did of him.

Lois respected Mary's taste in clothes, if not her artistic enthusiasms. After her husband and son returned, she wrote asking her sister-in-law to order two dresses for her in Paris. Mary consented willingly, though it meant interminable correspondence with Lois and equally extensive conferences with Armand, the French *couturier* of her choice. The dresses were eventually completed to specifications. One was of an expensive black material, trimmed with Spanish lace and "moonlight jet." The other was white crepe dotted with peach-pink rosebuds. Each cost 600 francs—far more than the Impressionists were getting for their paintings, when they sold at all.

Mary could not afford such expensive clothes for herself, but she took a great interest in them. Gratuitously, she gave Lois the fashion news that suede gloves were the latest thing and were worn even with white.

The Cassatts were having servant problems about this time. They discovered that their chef was adding a substantial commission to their grocery bills, and they fired him. For the two weeks they were without a cook, Mary's remarkable Alsatian maid, Mathilde Vallet, took over and surprised them with her culinary ability. Mathilde's skills were probably similar to those of her sister, Bertha, who, as Mary wrote her brother and sister-in-law, could dress hair, make hats and dresses, and iron flawlessly, and who spoke French extremely well, as most Alsatians did not, and also knew Italian and Arabic. The Alexander Cassatts finally brought this prodigy to America, to work for them at $5 a week, considered a "princely" salary at the time.

All these distractions did not keep Mary Cassatt from her painting. Two of her best portraits were done in 1882 and 1883. One of them, "Reading *Le Figaro*," was of her mother seated in a flowered armchair, wearing pince-nez glasses to read the French newspaper. "Monumentally conceived," Dr. Frederick Sweet of the Art Institute of Chicago would write of this picture of a tranquil elderly woman in a white dress, with the air of someone who had made peace with the world.

The other portrait, "Lady at the Tea Table," was of Mrs. Robert Moore Riddle, a cousin of Mrs. Cassatt. Mary apparently did it to repay some gifts that Mrs. Riddle had showered on them. It shows a stately dowager, hair parted in the middle and partially covered by a lace cap. The deep blue of her cape-dress is accented by her intense blue eyes and the blue of the Japanese porcelain tea set before her. The outline of her figure plays an integral role in the painting's design. Mary Cassatt had achieved mastery of the "lines" that Ingres and Degas so loved, using them in her own individual manner.

This portrait has a curious history. Although Degas said

"Lady at the Tea Table," Mary Cassatt. *The Metropolitan Museum of Art, gift of the Artist, 1923.*

it was "distinction itself," Mrs. Riddle refused it because her daughter, Mrs. Thomas Alexander Scott, felt her mother's nose was too large. "They are not very artistic," Mrs. Cassatt said of her two relatives in a letter to Alexander. For years the portrait lay forgotten in a storeroom. Mrs. Henry Havemeyer (the former Louisine Elder) came across it in 1914 and showed it to Paul Durand-Ruel. It made a sensation when he exhibited it. Mary gave it to the Metropolitan Museum in 1923.

Increasingly, Mary was turning to children as models. They might wiggle and squirm when she tried to draw them but at least they did not complain about the size of their noses. Mrs. Cassatt described one of them in a letter to her grandchild Katherine, on January 21, 1885, as "a little thing only two and a half years old, pretending to sew." Of all Mary Cassatt's work, nothing brought more rapturous comment than her treatment of youngsters.

In 1888, Edward Cassatt returned to Paris to enter the French military academy at St. Cyr. He was a young man now, wealthy and personable, and through his classmates met the elite of Paris. One letter home described a state dinner at the home of a Vicomtesse with "powdered footmen in livery everywhere." He still was a frequent visitor at the apartment of his grandparents and his Aunt Mary, and in another letter he gave a picture of Mary in the unlikely role of matchmaker.

A certain Captain Ballore dined with them. Aunt Mary had invited a friend named Mollie Riedner, for whom she had been trying to find an eligible suitor, to meet him. As Eddie was leaving his aunt rushed after him, saying proudly, "It has taken! He is head over heels in love with her!"

"Mrs. Gardner Cassatt and Her Baby," Mary Cassatt. Courtesy of the Library of Congress.

8

Berthe Morisot—A Friendly Rival

Paul Gauguin, on seeing the work of Mary Cassatt and Berthe Morisot side by side at an Impressionist exhibition, commented, "Mademoiselle Cassatt has just as much charm but more force." Another art authority claimed that Berthe Morisot was more subtle and had more spontaneity than Mary Cassatt. Because they were the only women who exhibited with the Impressionists (aside from Madame Braquemond, who only occasionally displayed her work), they were constantly being compared to each

102

other, usually to the detriment of one or the other. They had every reason to be jealous. This did not happen, at least perceptibly.

In any case they shared the distinction of being the finest women painters in France, or in America or anywhere else for that matter. It would have been difficult to name any woman who had surpassed them in the past. Each had an individual style.

Berthe Morisot preferred to work outdoors in the bright sunlight. Interior scenes were Mary Cassatt's forte, at least until her later years. Both liked pastels and both worked in oils, but Mary also liked the incisiveness of dry-point etchings, whereas Berthe Morisot experimented briefly with engraving but preferred the more fluid medium of watercolors. Mary prided herself on her "lines" —on the bold outlines of the figures in her compositions. In her treatment of light and color, Berthe Morisot adhered to Impressionist techniques.

Both came from moderately well-to-do families and neither ever had to worry about money. While for the Cassatts, culture was something to be acquired with great effort, culture for the Morisots was an integral part of their world. Mary Cassatt had to defy her father and the customs of her society to become an artist. Berthe Morisot's artistic leanings were encouraged and fostered by her parents. But in spite of differences in character and background, there were several striking parallels in the pattern of their lives.

Berthe Morisot, who was four years older than Mary Cassatt, was born in Bourges, the daughter of a government official. The family moved to Paris when she was small. In her early teens she began taking drawing lessons with her sisters, Yves and Edma, under an elderly painter, Father Chochard. Yves soon dropped out. Edma and

Berthe continued their art studies under a Beaux-Arts professor, Monsieur Guichard. When Mary Cassatt was a schoolgirl of fourteen, Berthe and her sister were copying the masters in the Louvre.

In 1860, when the Civil War put an end to Mary's dream of studying art in Rome, the Morisot sisters had already decided they did not care for Academic art. They went to the landscape painter Corot, and begged him to teach them to paint from nature. Corot turned them over to a disciple, since he did not give lessons himself, but he gave them advice and ended up as a close friend of their family and a frequent dinner guest. Berthe later destroyed all the paintings done under Corot's influence. Edma eventually gave up art to get married. Berthe remained dedicated to her work.

In 1863 Berthe visited the Salon des Refusés, where Napoleon III had ordered the display of all the paintings rejected by the Salon jury. In her opinion the most outstanding painting there was "Déjeuner sur l'Herbe" by Édouard Manet, which received the vilest abuse. Her sympathy was aroused for this artist whom she did not meet until several years later. She was already an unusually mature young woman of charm and distinction, with dark hair, large dark eyes, and a flawless complexion. The critic Théodore Duret spoke of her "gracious and natural manner." Manet had noticed her copying paintings at the Louvre, without knowing who she was.

About her own work, she was consistently modest. "I work hard, without pause, but all I do is absolutely waste," she said. Yet in 1864, when she was only twenty-three, the Salon accepted one of her paintings. That was the same year Mary Cassatt quit the Pennsylvania Academy, still uncertain in which direction her own talents lay.

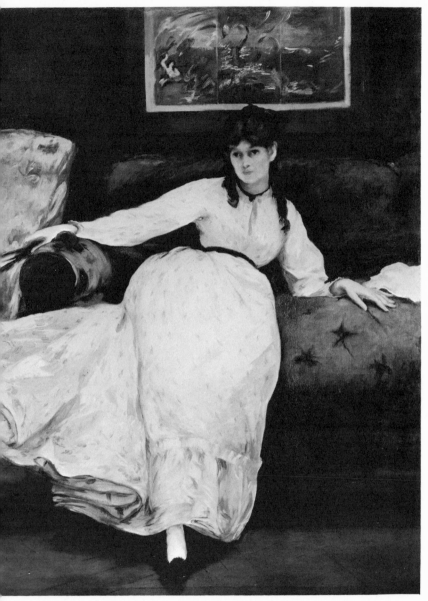

"Le Repos" (portrait of Berthe Morisot), Édouard Manet.
Museum of Art, Rhode Island School of Design.

Berthe Morisot finally met Édouard Manet through a fellow artist, Théodore Fantin-Latour. Manet was nine years older than she, just as Degas was nine years older than Mary Cassatt. From then on Berthe Morisot looked to Manet as her adviser, much as Mary Cassatt looked to Degas.

These two men, whom the two most talented women artists of their time chose as their guides and mentors, also had much in common. Like Degas' father, Manet's father, a prosperous judge, wanted him to study law. Manet rebelled and went to sea as a cadet on a freighter to Brazil. People later would refer to his "sailor's gait." On his return, with his father's consent, he studied art under Thomas Couture, an Academic artist. Couture contemptuously compared him to Honoré Daumier, esteemed today for his caricatures of the rich and powerful and his compassionate paintings of the poor. Manet took Couture's intended insult as a compliment. He resolved henceforth to paint only from real life, not realizing the trouble this decision would bring him.

"Manet is desperate because he is unable to paint atrocious pictures," Degas said of him.

Renoir once compared the two of them: "The incomprehensible thing is that Manet, so gentle and affectionate, was always attacked, whereas Degas, so vitriolic, violent and uncompromising, was accepted from the very first by the Academy, the public, and the revolutionaries."

Both were upper-class Parisians, men of the world at ease in any society, but Manet was far less temperamental and more affable and genial. He was happily married to a Dutch musician named Suzanne and was always popular with women. Aside from Mary Cassatt, Degas had only two or three close women friends. His most intimate friends were men.

"Self-Portrait," Édouard Manet. The Bettmann Archive.

Soon after Manet met Berthe Morisot, he asked her to pose as one of the three models in his painting "The Balcony" (Le Balcon). She agreed and appeared at his studio every day chaperoned by her mother. Of her own portrait in this painting, she commented, "I appear strange, rather than ugly." Nonetheless she continued to pose for him in other works. He preferred her to more conventionally pretty professional models. For similar reasons, Degas also liked to use Mary Cassatt as a model.

As in the case of Mary Cassatt and Degas, there has been considerable speculation about Berthe Morisot's personal relationship with Manet. From her letters to her sister one can guess that she was a little in love with him, at least for a time. "I find in him a charming nature which pleases me infinitely," she wrote. But it was his brother Eugène, a tall handsome young man who posed for one of the men in "Déjeuner sur l'Herbe," whom she married when she was thirty-three. "I cannot pity myself since I have found a fine husband who I believe loves me sincerely," she told a friend. Her devotion to Édouard Manet as a friend and as an artist remained as strong as ever after her marriage. The brothers and their wives saw each other frequently.

Shortly after her marriage, she stopped submitting to the Salon and decided to throw her lot in with the Impressionists. When Professor Guichard, her former teacher, saw her works at what he called the "pernicious surroundings" of the First Impressionist Exhibition, he was outraged. "One associates with madmen at grave peril," he wrote Berthe Morisot's mother. Manet also opposed her joining the Impressionists, no doubt feeling it would not help her reputation, but for once she would not listen to him. Her ruthless treatment at the hands of the critics of the First Exhibition has already been mentioned, but like Mary Cassatt, she was not daunted at having her name linked with these rebel, outcast artists.

Although Édouard Manet would not exhibit with them, he had gradually come to like them and admire their work. When a visitor came to see him, he pointed out the pictures on his walls, exclaiming, "Look at that Renoir! Look at that Monet! Look at that Degas! How talented they are, these friends of mine."

Several times he helped Monet out of his financial difficulties, and once, when Madame Monet was still living, spent several weeks with the Monets at Argenteuil. The two men painted together in the garden, using Madame Monet and her firstborn son, Jean, as models. Briefly, Manet experimented with Impressionist techniques. The brighter colors of his later works show the Impressionist influence.

All Berthe Morisot's fellow artists loved and respected her. When later disputes broke out among their group, she was the force that held them together. She was fond of them all and never took sides. In her home on the rue Paul Valéry, she held open house for *avant-garde* artists, writers, and musicians. Monet, Renoir and his wife, Pissarro—the patriarch of the Impressionists—and Degas were all frequent visitors. Berthe Morisot liked creative people and was indifferent to their social station.

If Mary Cassatt sensed that some of her colleagues felt warmer toward her gentle rival than they did to her, she did not let it bother her. Americans could consider her eccentric because she was an artist, and the French might consider her eccentric because she was an American, but it was all the same to her. What people called a normal life for a woman—being a wife and mother—still did not tempt her. She hardly thought of herself as a woman at all, only as an artist.

Sometime in the early 1880's, Eugène Manet wrote his wife that Miss Cassatt had expressed an interest in becoming closer friends with them. He added that he found this an excellent idea. Berthe Morisot accepted her overtures graciously and seems to have become attached to her, though their friendship always retained a certain formality.

They attended art exhibitions together. Berthe Morisot once sent Mary Cassatt a corsage, which she wore to a concert. Through Berthe Morisot she met a number of creative people in fields outside of art. One of them was the poet Stéphane Mallarmé, whose "Afternoon of a Faun" (L'Après-midi d'un Faune) inspired Debussy's orchestral work of that name and who was christened an "Impressionist poet" by Victor Hugo.

When Berthe Morisot heard that Mallarmé was going to see Mary Cassatt, she sent her best wishes to her American friend. Mallarmé reported back that Mademoiselle Cassatt seemed to count on her greatly.

Mary Cassatt once proposed that she and Berthe Morisot do portraits of each other, but somehow they never did. They admired each other's work sincerely, though neither influenced the other. It will be remembered that one of the early purchases Mary Cassatt forced on Alexander was Berthe Morisot's "River Scene."

A strong bond between them, possibly unspoken, was that they were both in a field hitherto almost barred to women. Neither had totally escaped the wounds of male chauvinism, even among their colleagues. Mary Cassatt frequently objected when Degas modified his praise by saying she painted very well—for a woman.

Édouard Manet also exhibited a touch of male superiority. Soon after he met Berthe and Edma Morisot, he wrote a friend that the Morisot sisters were very charming, adding, with his own brand of humor, that "as women, they could further the cause of painting if each was to marry an Academician and sow the seeds of discord in the ranks of that rotten lot." One can hope that Berthe Morisot never learned of this flippant letter. She would not have been amused. Manet did hurt her feelings once by excusing himself from showing her around an exhibition on the grounds that he "was not a nursemaid."

It was probably through Berthe and Eugène Manet that Mary Cassatt came to be on visiting terms with Édouard Manet and his wife. Her esteem for Manet had been growing, not because of his controversial subject matter, but because of his vivid color contrasts, his skilled juxtaposition of light and shadow, and his decisive composition. She ranked him with Degas and Courbet as the greatest of modern painters. Oddly enough, though she looked to Degas for guidance, it was Manet who most influenced her own style—more so in fact than he ever influenced Berthe Morisot.

When Mary Cassatt met him, Édouard Manet was no longer the debonair figure of his youth. Locomotor ataxia, a disease of the nervous system, kept him in excruciating pain most of the time, but he refused to stop working. "Le Bar aux Folies-Bergère," a lighthearted scene of a pretty maid in a cabaret, was done while he was in agony. It was a great triumph at the Salon of 1882 and resulted in Manet's winning the Legion of Honor, France's highest award.

Mary Cassatt took Louisine Elder to see him that summer in the Paris suburb of Rueil, but Berthe Morisot met them at the door and said he was too ill to see anyone. Within a few months his left leg became infected with gangrene, which an amputation failed to arrest. He died in April 1883, at the age of fifty.

"Boating," Édouard Manet. The Metropolitan Museum of Art, H. O. Havemeyer Collection, bequest of Mrs. H. O. Havemeyer, 1929.

At his funeral Émile Zola, Claude Monet, and the critic Théodore Duret served as pallbearers. Mary Cassatt may have been among the five-hundred-odd mourners in the funeral procession. To her sister Edma, Berthe Morisot wrote: "On his funeral day everyone who attended, instead of appearing indifferent as people usually are on such occasions, seemed to me like one big family mourning one of their own."

Ever since the Franco-Prussian War, Paul Durand-Ruel had given his moral and financial support to the Impresssionists. In 1884 he found himself on the verge of financial ruin, unable to buy their paintings at any price. "I should like to be free to go away and live in a desert," he wrote Pissarro. Mary Cassatt came to his rescue with a loan to tide him over. She was also at least in part responsible for an invitation from the American Art Association for Durand-Ruel to organize an exhibition of Impressionist painters in New York City. The Durand-Ruel name was already known in America. The Barbizon painters his father had launched there were now commanding large sums. Durand-Ruel saw the invitation as a chance to recover his losses and open a new market.

Not all the Impressionists were as hopeful. "I should be sorry to see some of my paintings go to Yankee-land," wrote Monet. ". . . Paris is the one and only place where there is still good taste." But the artist Fantin-Latour insisted Americans were not savages: "On the contrary they are less ignorant and less conservative than art lovers in France."

In all, Durand-Ruel assembled some three hundred canvases for his American exhibition, advertised as "Works in Oils and Pastels by the Impressionists of Paris." The first major showing of its kind, it opened in New York on April 10, 1886. The reluctant Monet had fifty paintings on display, and there were others by Pissarro, Degas, Eugène Boudin, Édouard Manet, and Berthe Morisot. Mary Cassatt was represented by two paintings loaned by Alexander, "Family Group" and "Portrait of a Lady."

The large numbers of Americans who attended the exhibition daily showed no trace of the mockery of Parisian art lovers. Clearly, Fantin-Latour was justified in his belief that Americans were not savages. Some $18,000 worth of paintings were sold, which for those days meant success. *The New York Daily Tribune* gave special credit to Mary Cassatt for her "untiring efforts in drawing the attention of her countrymen to the merits of her French colleagues." Though most art reviews were favorable, praise for her as the one American artist represented was noticeably scant.

On May 15, 1886, almost simultaneously with the American showing, the Eighth—and last—Impressionist Exhibition opened in Paris. Under the urgent persuasion of Pissarro and of Berthe Morisot and her husband, Mary Cassatt and Degas, who had boycotted the last exhibition, agreed to join with them. To avoid any wrangling about their name, the exhibition was announced simply as the Eighth Exposition of Painting.

Degas submitted some pastels of milliners, including the one for which Mary Cassatt had posed, along with a series of nudes in everyday poses, bathing themselves, combing their hair, performing their toilette. Mary Cassatt's most striking offering was "Girl Arranging Her Hair" (La Toilette Matinale), showing a homely, red-haired girl in a white chemise sitting in front of a washstand. Degas was fascinated by this oil, which admittedly has more appeal for connoisseurs than for popular taste, and bought it for himself.

It was understood that Degas, Berthe Morisot, and

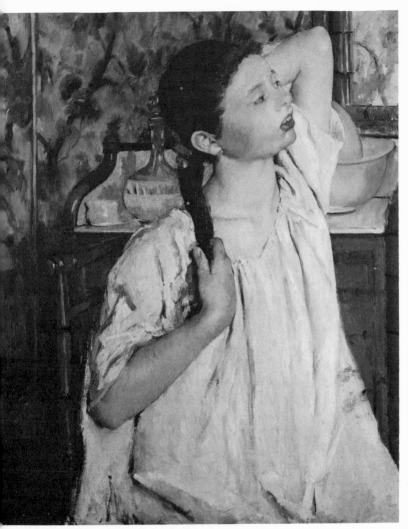

"Girl Arranging Her Hair," Mary Cassatt. National Gallery of Art, Washington, D.C., Chester Dale Collection.

Mary Cassatt should bear most of the exhibition expenses, as they had done before. Degas took this as a matter of course, and to Berthe Morisot it seemed perfectly normal that the more affluent artists should pay the share of the others. Mary Cassatt had never objected and did not do so now, but inwardly she was irritated. Was it possible that her colleagues included her only because she was supposed to be a rich American? The seed of this unreasoning suspicion would grow slowly in the years to come until she turned against everything French.

Most of the critical and public attention at the exhibition was focused not on the oldtimers but on two young men Pissarro had insisted his comrades should accept— Paul Signac and Georges Seurat. They had adopted a technique of constructing their compositions by means of innumerable dots of pure color, mixed with white for luminosity. They were called "Pointillists" because of these myriads of "points" of color, but later they would be known as founders of Neo-Impressionism, the first of many art movements that would follow in the wake of Impressionism. But it was the Impressionists who started the trend away from conventional art.

In 1886, the same year as the eighth exhibition, Émile Zola published a novel called *The Masterpiece* (L'Oeuvre), the story of an artist who went mad trying to paint a perfect picture. In essence it was a satire on the long and painful struggle of the Impressionists for recognition. Moreover, the hero bore striking resemblance to Paul Cézanne, with whom Zola had grown up in Aix-en-Provence. Cézanne, who had trusted Zola implicitly, seems to have been stunned on learning through this book that Zola really considered him a failure. Zola sent him a copy, for which Cézanne thanked him, but the two men never met again.

"View of the Port of Marseilles," Paul Signac. *The Metropolitan Museum of Art, gift of Robert Lehman, 1955.*

"A Sunday Afternoon on the Island of La Grande Jatte," Georges Seurat. Courtesy of the Art Institute of Chicago.

Monet and Pissarro took *L'Oeuvre* as an act of betrayal
on the part of Zola. They felt that in spite of the support
he had given them he had never had any conception of
what their art was about. They did not forgive him for a
long time. The feelings of Mary Cassatt and Berthe Morisot in this controversy are not recorded, but certainly they
must have sided with Cézanne and their colleagues.

In March 1887 the Cassatts moved to a new apartment,
at 10 rue Marignan, just off the boulevard de Champs-
Élysées. It was more spacious and more elegant than their
previous one, with quarters for their servants in the attic
above the apartment. The furniture was a careless mixture of Louis XV, Louis XVI, First Empire, and Second
Empire. One visitor described the general effect as "stuffy
French-Victorian" and remarked that there were fringes
on everything—on curtains, draperies, lamps, and table-
cloths. Only the colorful paintings on the walls saved the
apartment from gloom. Mary's collection now included
Courbet and Manet, in addition to the works of Degas
and the Impressionists. She would keep the rue de Marignan apartment until her death.

In their new quarters the Cassatts entertained more frequently and more lavishly than ever before. Most of their
guests were Americans abroad, but there was also a select
group of Mary's French friends. The poet Mallarmé was
a regular caller. Another visitor was Clemenceau, whom
Mary had first met at a breakfast party in 1884; he was
now a member of the French Chambre des Députés, a
deputy in France being the equivalent of an American
congressman. A born politician, he was also a man of the
widest range of cultural and scholarly interests. His passion was Greek art and history. He adored Monet and the
other Impressionists, and his enthusiasm for modern
French art extended to include the works of Mary Cassatt.

She now kept her own horse in a Paris stable. Riding was still her greatest relaxation. Frequently, after a ride through the Bois de Boulogne, she stopped by to see Berthe Morisot, who had become a widow in 1886. Her little daughter Julie welcomed those visits; to her great delight Mary Cassatt would let her mount her horse and gallop around their large garden.

These outings came to an end in the summer of 1888. While out riding with her father, Mary fell from her horse, breaking her right leg and dislocating her left shoulder. She would never be able to ride again. "Tillet must have written you that poor Mlle. Cassatt had a fall from her horse," Degas wrote his friend, Henri Rouart. "Here she is . . . immobilized for many long summer weeks and then cut off from active life and perhaps also from her passion as a horsewoman."

Mary's reaction was chiefly embarrassment at what she considered a stupid and silly accident.

After her recovery she continued to see Berthe Morisot at intervals, though perhaps not as frequently as before. Berthe Morisot had long been in poor health, as a result of privations during the 1870 siege of Paris, and she became prematurely white-haired. "As I grow older, painting seems to me more difficult and more useless," she once said sadly. It seems evident that she never appreciated her own worth, never thought her efforts worthwhile, though she continued painting until her death in 1895.

She left behind her a legacy of paintings in which anyone, man or woman, could take pride. Her work conveys the exuberance of nature. She loved flowers and trees and the greenery of gardens. Her favorite model was her little daughter Julie, who was lovely as a flower herself. "Surely the freshest exhibition in New York at the moment is Berthe Morisot's," wrote John Canaday of *The New York*

Times about a 1960 showing, "although this enchanting Impressionist died sixty-five years ago."

Her name and Mary Cassatt's are still linked together, in France and America, as the outstanding women artists of the Impressionist period, and outstanding in their own right, regardless of their sex.

9

The Japanese Influence, Pissarro, and "the Patriots"

One of the exhibitions Mary Cassatt and Berthe Morisot attended together was a large showing of Japanese art, held at the Paris École des Beaux-Arts in April and May of 1890. Mary went once with Edgar Degas, again with Berthe Morisot, and possibly other times on her own. Some 725 Japanese color prints, more than 350 books, and an assortment of Japanese *objets d'art* were on display. The prints interested Mary the most.

The Western world had become aware of Japanese art

only in the last several decades. When Commodore Matthew Perry sailed to Japan in 1853, he negotiated America's first commercial treaty with that isolated country; this paved the way for the first Japanese exports. Three years later the French engraver Auguste Delâtre found a small volume of woodcuts by Hokusai, the Japanese landscapist, in the packing of a porcelain shipment. Other Western artists saw them and marveled. The critic Théodore Duret, who toured the Orient in 1873, claimed that the Japanese were the first and finest Impressionists.

Degas had often talked to Mary about how talented the Japanese artists were, how much they could convey through simple lines, and how superbly they used color and masses in their compositions. Her own enthusiasm did not catch fire until she saw the 1890 exhibit. Over the next years she acquired a number of landscapes by Hiroshige and Hokusai and figure prints by Kiyonaga, Shunjo, Utamaro, and Yeisih. A more immediate effect of her Japanese discovery was a series of ten color prints that she did in 1890 and 1891. These prints show clearly the Japanese influence in their lines and color harmonies, which she adapted, however, to her own subject matter and themes, and for which she worked out her own techniques.

To make their prints, the Japanese used wood blocks— a different block for each color and one for the lines. Mary had had no experience with wood blocks, and she made her prints from copper engravings.

Her engraving up until now had been principally a work discipline, to improve her drawing skills. Her first two or three prints had been straight etching; then she had switched to soft ground, aquatint, and drypoint. (Whereas straight etching is done with a pointed steel cutting tool called a burin, drypoint is done with a special needle that raises a burr on both sides of the line.)

For her series of Japanese-influenced color prints, which were not a "work discipline" but works of art, she made use of all the techniques she had mastered earlier. First she drew an outline in drypoint on a copper plate. She then transferred this outline by tracing paper to two or three other plates, depending on how many colors she planned to use. Next, she sprinkled the section to be colored on each plate with a powdered rosin, slightly heated so that it would adhere to the plate and form a hard, granular surface. She applied color to each print *à la poupée*, that is, by using little "dolls" of rags.

For the actual printing, she worked alongside of her printer, checking each proof to make certain that the overlay of color and line was absolutely accurate. She was so exceedingly meticulous about this that sometimes they put in an eight-hour day and produced no more than eight or ten proofs that satisfied her. After twenty-five impressions were made of each print, the plates were discarded.

Her choice of colors was her own. She did not use black, which the Impressionists had barred from their palette. Pissarro, in a letter to his artist son, Lucien, spoke of her "adorable blues" and "fresh rose." She also liked shades of brown and tan, grey, green, and yellow.

She used her favorite mother-and-child theme in several of the prints. The majority were studies of women alone. One of the latter was "Woman Bathing" (La Toilette). In it, a woman with a striped robe tied around her waist is leaning over a washbasin. The deep blue wall of the background accents the blue tone of the patterned rug.

"I would not admit that a woman could draw that well!" exclaimed Degas, the first time he saw "La Toilette."

Mary Cassatt might have retorted that there was no rea-

"The Bath," Mary Cassatt. *Courtesy of the Library of Congress.*

son under heaven why a woman should not draw as well as any man, but it would have been useless. She might argue with him but she could never change him.

Another of these prints, alternately titled "In the Tramway," "In the Omnibus," and "In the Boat," shows a mother seated on a bench next to a nursemaid, who holds a baby on her lap. The window in back of them gives a glimpse of a river and a bridge. The bench is dark blue and the shoreline along the river is turquoise. The gowns of the women are in shades of tan. The baby wears a billowing white dress and white bonnet, which in outline resemble an exotic flower. The print conveys a mood of tranquility. Whether on streetcar, bus, or boat, the two women passengers are caught in the transient relaxation familiar to all voyagers, freed from tensions or problems they left behind and which may await them at the end of their journey.

The Japanese influence is evident in all the ten prints —in some more strongly than in others. The model in "The Letter," who is sitting at a desk sealing an envelope, has the lacquered hair of a Japanese woman of fashion, and her eyes are slightly slanted. The Oriental atmosphere is further accentuated by the delicately flowered wallpaper. Each of the prints has its own charm. The series was one of Mary Cassatt's finest achievements.

In the opinion of Adelyn D. Breeskin of the Smithsonian Institution, if the color prints were Mary Cassatt's sole accomplishment, they would give her just claim to fame. "They now stand as her most original contribution," Mrs. Breeskin writes, "adding a new chapter to the history of graphic arts . . . technically, as color prints, they have never been surpassed."

She was in the midst of the intense creative labor which the prints involved when she received a singular blow to

"In the Omnibus" (In the Tramway; In the Boat), Mary
Cassatt. S. P. Avery Collection, Prints Division, The New
York Public Library, Astor, Lenox, and Tilden Foundations.

"The Letter," Mary Cassatt. Courtesy of the Library of Congress.

her pride as an engraver. In 1891 a group of modern French artists, including some Mary Cassatt knew very well, organized under the name of Society of French Painter-Engravers (Société des Peintres-Graveurs Français) and announced an exhibition at the Durand-Ruel gallery. The Society ruled out foreign-born artists in their membership. As an American, Mary Cassatt was automatically excluded.

The white-bearded patriarch of the Impressionists, Camille Pissarro, was also ineligible for the Society's exhibition, since he had been born in the West Indies, the son of a Portuguese Jew and a Creole mother. Being wholly dependent on sales of his works to support himself and his family, he was even more unhappy about the situation than Mary was. He visited her several times that spring to win her over to a plan he had conceived—that he and she should hold separate exhibitions at the same time as the Society held its own.

Mary was very doubtful about his proposal at first. A perfectionist, she had never felt herself ready for a one-man show. But she had confidence in Pissarro's judgment and finally let herself be persuaded that holding separate exhibitions would be one way of righting an injustice that had been done to them.

Pissarro and Mary Cassatt shared a love for engraving. Both were dedicated to art, and selfless in the support of other artists in whom they believed. Nevertheless, their outside interests were so different that it is almost surprising they became such good friends.

It was not only that Pissarro was a landscape painter and that Mary preferred portraits. Or that his models were working-class people and hers were of her own social class. Pissarro had never been free of financial worries since he came to Paris from the West Indies in his early

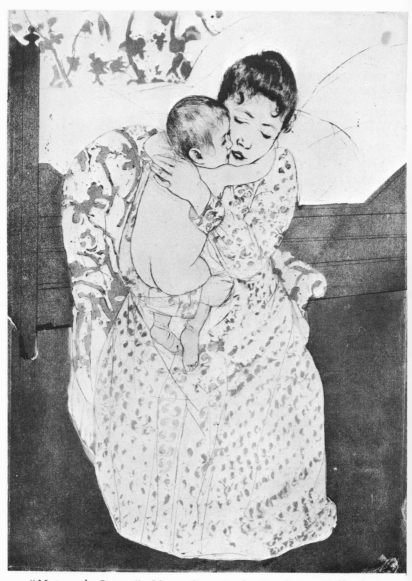

"Maternal Caress," Mary Cassatt. S. P. Avery Collection, Prints Division, The New York Public Library, Astor, Lenox, and Tilden Foundations.

twenties. With five children to bring up, he was constantly at the end of his rope. Nor did he have the solace of a sympathetic wife, as did Renoir, or as had Monet far too briefly. Madame Pissarro, to put it charitably, never could understand why her husband wasted time painting when there was no profit in it. Mary Cassatt, on the other hand, did not know what it meant to have a family to support. She never needed to worry where the next meal was coming from.

Pissarro fought injustice wherever he found it. The most radical of the Impressionists, he was a Socialist and for a period an Anarchist—words that were highly shocking to many of Mary's Philadelphia friends. What the critic Claude Roger-Marx called his "tender humanity" extended not only to oppressed workers and peasants but to anyone who was mistreated.

In the early days of the Impressionist exhibitions he got into a fist fight with an anti-Impressionist who had referred to Berthe Morisot as a streetwalker. Hard pressed as he was, Pissarro always found time to encourage and launch young artists of talent. Cézanne, Gauguin, Seurat, Signac, and Vincent van Gogh were among those whose abilities he recognized long before anyone else.

He did not need to launch Mary Cassatt. She had done that by herself, with the aid of Degas. For once, Pissarro was in the position of receiving as much as he gave. When he confided that Durand-Ruel was no longer handling his work, she was aghast; she promised to put pressure on that dealer and to intensify her efforts to sell his paintings and engravings to her American friends. His radical politics did not deter her. In fact, her own political thinking in later years may have stemmed from their talks together.

While she sympathized with his problems, she also found that she could open her heart to him about her

own. With this kindly man she could be confident, as she
was not with Degas, that he would never say anything to
hurt her. He was impressed by her Japanese-influenced
prints and the techniques she had evolved to make them.

"You remember the effects you strove for at Eragny?"
Pissarro wrote his son Lucien in London. "Well, Miss
Cassatt has realized just such effects, and admirably: the
tone even, subtle, delicate, without stains on seams . . . .
I have seen attempts at color engraving which will appear
in the exhibition of the patriots, but the work is ugly,
heavy, lusterless and commercial . . . ."

"Patriots" was Pissarro's name for the exclusive Society
of French Painter-Engravers.

His and Mary Cassatt's exhibitions opened at the same
time as the Society's in two small rooms adjoining the
main Durand-Ruel gallery, where the larger exhibition
was held. Pissarro foresaw that their rivals would be
furious to discover a show "of rare and exquisite works"
next to their own. Mary Cassatt was less certain. She limited her showing to five paintings and twelve prints.

The day after the opening, she was invited to a dinner
held by the Society at the home of the sculptor Albert
Bartholomé. It is reported that they teased her so merci-
lessly for her attempt to get back at them that she was reduced to tears. But Degas at least stood up for her. He was
charmed, he said, "by the noble element in her work."

In a letter to Alexander, Mrs. Cassatt wrote that both
critics and collectors had praised his sister's first one-man
show. Pissarro reported more gloomily to Lucien: "What
has befallen Miss Cassatt is just what I predicted: great indifference on the part of the visitors and even much opposition . . . . As to the practical results which Miss Cassatt
anticipated, we must not count on them unduly . . . ."

If their success was not dazzling, they could console

themselves that at least they had not let "the patriots" keep their engravings from being seen. After their private exhibitions were over, Pissarro returned to his home at Eragny outside of Paris to continue his lonely struggle for survival, while Mary left for her summer vacation with her parents.

They had splurged this year and rented the eighteenth-century Château Bachivillers, set on a 1,500-acre estate some fifty miles north of Paris. Of red brick with gray stone trim, three stories high, with two-story wings at each side, the château had two salons, a dining room, a billiard room, and more bedrooms than they could ever use. The owner, a wealthy farmer, supplied them with all the fruit and vegetables they could eat and sold them milk at less than a penny a quart.

Mrs. Cassatt wrote Alexander in July that they had bought a new horse for their carriage. It turned out that he had a thin skin and flies drove him crazy. He had fallen when he turned around to bite them. One knee was sure to be scarred, which would lower his value. "Mary firmly believes she has bad luck," her mother said. Still she was busy painting, intent on "fame and money." An unmarried woman was fortunate if she loved her work, Mrs. Cassatt philosophized. The more absorbing the work, the better.

Mary was working on seven more color prints that summer. One of them, "Feeding the Ducks," which showed two women and a little girl in a boat with ducks clustered around them, was especially delightful. The impact of Oriental art had worn off. The Japanese influence is less apparent in these prints than in the earlier ones. Critics find them less forceful and compact than the original ten.

She did not forget Pissarro on her return to Paris in the fall. His prints and his canvases were regularly on display

"Feeding the Ducks," Mary Cassatt. The Metropolitan Museum of Art, H. O. Havemeyer Collection, bequest of Mrs. H. O. Havemeyer, 1929.

for her American guests. In November 1891 he wrote Lucien that he had received a letter from Miss Cassatt saying that she was coming to Eragny with an American friend who wanted to take lessons from him. Though his wife was away and he had no pretensions of being a cook, he had invited them to lunch. "Never mind, we shall do what we can."

Apparently his lunch was a success, for a few weeks later three more American women sent by Mary Cassatt came to Eragny to see him. They were looking for lodging in the neighborhood so that they could be near him and study under him. "You see, there will be a colony soon," Pissarro wrote his son.

Mary Cassatt was clearly trying to help him, but he turned the tables on her. He would not take her friends as paying students but gave them all the free advice they wanted.

10

Lady of the Château

While the Cassatts were vacationing at the Château Bachivillers in 1891, they took an excursion to see another château five miles distant, which was for sale.

Equally spacious as Bachivillers, the Château de Beaufresne, at Mesnil-Théribus, was set well back from the main road beyond a wide expanse of green lawn, framed at each side by curving driveways approaching it through borders of tall trees. It was a three-story building of rose-colored brick, each story separated by bands of white marble. At each side was a hexagonal tower. A pediment spanned the three central windows of the facade.

For Mary Cassatt, it was apparently love at first sight.

Beaufresne had been built in the seventeenth century as the hunting lodge on the grounds of a far larger mansion, long since in ruins. The present owners belonged to the noble De Grasse family, who traced their ancestry back to the Crusades. A more recent ancestor was Comte Paul de Grasse, a French admiral who had played a major role in the victory of Yorktown, the decisive battle in the American Revolution.

Once she made up her mind, Mary wasted no time getting in touch with the representatives of this distinguished family, so she could sign the papers that made the château her own. It could not have been expensive. French châteaus were then going for a song. She felt proud that she could pay for it out of her own money made from the sale of her paintings.

Like many ancient buildings not properly kept up, the Château de Beaufresne was badly in need of repairs and renovations. It would be two years before it would be habitable and the Cassatts could move in. Mr. Cassatt did not live to make this last change of address. After the family's summer vacation, he fell gravely ill, and he died on December 9, 1891. Mary's family abroad was now reduced to herself and her mother.

Although she was still far better known in France than in America, over the years she had acquired a few staunch American admirers. Among these was the very rich Mrs. Potter Palmer, whose husband owned a fortune in real estate, including the famous Palmer House Hotel in Chicago. Beautiful, energetic, and quite intelligent, Mrs. Palmer was the leader and arbiter of Chicago society. On one of her many trips abroad, she had met Mary Cassatt, who persuaded her to invest in Impressionist art. In the pseudo-medieval turreted castle in Chicago where the Potter Palmers lived in royal splendor, she installed a picture gallery for her acquisitions. Many of these would later be part of the Chicago Art Institute's impressive Impressionist collection.

In 1890 Congress authorized a commission to organize the World's Columbian Exposition, to be held on the shores of Lake Michigan from May to November 1893. Mrs. Palmer was appointed president of the Board of Lady Managers. She had long found it regrettable that such a fine artist as Mary Cassatt, a protégée of the great Degas, should be so relatively unknown in America. Now she felt herself in a position to do something to remedy the situation.

To house the Exposition, 150 buildings were erected in Romanesque style of a material resembling marble. One was the Woman's Building, for which a twenty-one-year-old Bostonian, Sophia B. Hayden, was the architect. It was agreed that only women artists should be chosen to decorate the interior of the building.

Mrs. Palmer spent the summer of 1891 in Europe, lavishly entertaining foreign diplomats and statesmen and using all her wiles to convince them to participate in the Chicago fair on a scale larger than they had envisaged. She took time off from these social obligations to visit Mary Cassatt and ask her to do a mural for a tympanum—the recessed space beneath a high arch—in the Woman's Building. The artist would not be obliged to come to Chicago herself and mount a scaffold to paint on the walls. She could paint a canvas of the proper size in her studio in France and ship it to America. A second tympanum was to be done by Mrs. Mary Fairchild MacMonnies, wife of the sculptor Frederick MacMonnies.

The Woman's Building, World's Columbian Exposition. Courtesy of the Chicago Historical Society.

Mary gave her consent partially to please Mrs. Palmer but even more because she was intrigued at the idea of experimenting in a new art form. It was a spur-of-the-moment decision, which she might have considered more carefully had she guessed the headaches involved.

In due time the contracts came through. Both Mary Cassatt and Mrs. MacMonnies were up in arms at the terms, which stipulated that they would not be paid until their work was completed and that they would have to install the murals at their own expense. Regretfully but firmly, they refused to sign until Mrs. Palmer could revise the contracts on more suitable terms.

Not until the summer of 1892 was Mary able to begin work on the mural. Her own château was filled with workmen. She and her mother were vacationing for the second time at the Château Bachivillers. Solely for this huge project, she had a large glass-roofed studio specially built in their garden. To avoid the need of working on a ladder, she devised an elaborate apparatus, made to order, that would lower her canvas into an excavation when she needed to work on the upper section.

There were a multitude of other technical problems to be solved. Since the tympanum was rounded at the top, she could not place the canvas against a straight wall but had to have special stretchers made. She was not informed of the exact size of the tympanum until September. It would have saved her a good deal of extra work if she had known this at the beginning, she wrote Mrs. Palmer, adding tactfully that "it would be ungracious to grumble."

Somewhere along the line she learned that the mural would be placed some forty-eight feet high. She was overcome with consternation. If people ignored paintings hung in the third tier of the Salon galleries, how would they feel about straining their necks to gaze at art as high as the fourth floor of an average Paris apartment build-ing? But there was nothing she could do about it, and it was too late to back out.

To minimize the hazard of being overlooked altogether, she decided to make her figures near life-size, set off with a border at the top and bottom. A young man came out from Paris to work on the borders. He was so slow that Mary took over the job herself, "hammer and tongs." She had to hire a gilder to put in gold where required. This did not take long but "cost like the mischief."

Since the mural would be placed in the Woman's Building, she appropriately took "Modern Woman" as her theme. She treated this subject in a series of allegories, but avoided any resemblance to the Salon-type paintings of mythology by having all her models in modern dress.

The center and largest composition showed young women plucking the fruits of "Knowledge and Science." One of the side panels was called "Arts, Music, and Danc-ing," and showed young women painting, playing instru-ments, and doing dances. The other panel, titled "Young Girls Pursuing Fame," presented Fame as an elusive winged creature. Since all three scenes were outdoors, Mary was free to use brilliant colors. She did her best to create a totally modern atmosphere, "as bright, as gay, as amusing as possible." The Japanese influence still showed in the simplicity of her lines. Her growing interest in Per-sian art was reflected in the intricate pattern of the border design.

She was still at the Château Bachivillers, hard at work, in December 1892 when Paul Durand-Ruel came to see her. Following the success of his 1886 exhibition in Amer-ica, he had opened a gallery on Fifth Avenue, in a build-ing owned by Henry O. Havemeyer, who with his wife (the former Louisine Elder) had become his best custom-

"*Modern Woman*" (*central panel*), *Mary Cassatt. Courtesy of the Chicago Historical Society.*

ers of Impressionist art. His fortune restored, Durand-Ruel was now back in France to try to recapture some of his artists who had gone to other dealers in his absence.

Mary Cassatt showed him the mural panels she was working on. He was, in her words, "kind and encouraging" and said he would buy them if they were for sale. The careful work she had put into the murals amazed him. But then he had never seen the frescoes of the early Italian masters, she wrote Mrs. Palmer. It was that sort of perfection in detail that she was striving for.

The compliments of Durand-Ruel, pleasing as they were, were not what she needed. A dozen times she was on the verge of asking Degas to come judge her work, but she never did. She felt that should he arrive in one of his sarcastic moods, he would "demolish" her so completely she never would get finished in time for the Exposition. In truth, he might well have found hilarious the very idea of a bunch of women decorating an imitation marble palace in the wilds of Chicago.

Without Degas' advice, and in spite of her fears, her finished panels reached Chicago in plenty of time for the opening of the Exposition. The reaction there was mixed. Some of Mrs. Potter Palmer's Board of Lady Managers felt her conception of "Modern Woman" was inaccurate. The official Exposition publication commented politely that Mary Cassatt's large painting would be remembered by many visitors, notwithstanding the inconvenient height at which it was placed.

A strongly favorable article about Mary Cassatt as an artist, written by Miss Sara Hallowell, appeared in "Art and Handicraft in the Woman's Building of the World's Columbian Exposition." With her strong lines and exquisite colors, she was easily the best of American women painters, it said. The Luxembourg Museum in Paris had purchased a set of her etchings. The French Government had invited her to present it with a picture, "an honor which falls to few," but Miss Cassatt had "characteristically" declined.

Miss Hallowell said little about the murals, however, and Maud Howe Elliot, who wrote about her in the same publication, limited herself mostly to describing the panels. Their allegorical nature apparently missed her. She referred to the largest composition as a picture of young women gathering apples in a pleasant orchard. The border was charming, Miss Elliott conceded, and the children on it were beautifully painted.

For all the time, energy, and anxiety Mary Cassatt had given the mural, there is little evidence that it did much to enhance her reputation in America. Nor did the public ever have the chance to see it at a more convenient height, for it was destroyed after the fair when the Exposition buildings were torn down.

Back in Paris, Mary was busy getting ready for her second one-man show, which was held at the Durand-Ruel galleries in November and December 1893. It was far larger and far more impressive than her first show with Pissarro. Ninety-eight of her works were on display, including seventeen paintings, fourteen pastels, and a wide assortment of prints. Among the paintings were "A Cup of Tea" and "The Cup of Tea," "At the Opera" (À l'Opéra), "The Bath" (La Toilette de l'Enfant), and "Girl Arranging Her Hair" (La Toilette), which Degas had bought after it was shown at the Eighth Impressionist Exhibition. All these are now in American museums.

The exhibition was a great success. "One must admit in all sincerity that Miss Cassatt is perhaps, besides Whistler, the only great and distinguished artist which America now possesses," wrote André Mellario in his introduction

"At the Opera," Mary Cassatt. *Courtesy of the Museum of Fine Arts, Boston.*

to her catalog. Critics were no less eulogistic. French collectors demanded more and more of her works and paid good prices for them.

When her exhibition closed, she and her mother took a vacation at Cap d'Antibes on the warm and sunny Riviera. Her brother Gardner and his family joined them. She painted a portrait of young Gardner, Jr., "Boy in the Sailor Suit." He did not enjoy posing and once spit in her face. His mother punished him by shutting him in a closet. Mary Cassatt promptly drove off to town in her carriage and returned with a box of chocolates for him.

That period at Antibes was a creative one for her. It was as though she had thrown off the shackles that the Chicago mural had fastened on her, along with an inner feeling that for all her work it was no more than a pleasant decoration. Now once again she could paint as she wanted to paint, using canvases of a size that pleased her and that were best suited to the intricate and intimate harmony of her compositions.

At this time she did "The Boating Party," which shows a woman with a small boy on her lap in the bow of a boat, facing the boatman at the oars. It is said that "The Boating Party" was inspired by Manet's "In the Boat," done in 1874. Though the figures are different, there is the same deep blue of the water, the same clear-cut outline and design.

A pastel done at this time was "Woman Arranging Her Veil," which people said had a French elegance. The Persian influence came to the fore in another lovely pastel, "In the Garden." Here, her mother and child models are almost submerged in an intricate patterned background in the fashion of Persian miniatures. She liked pastels, a medium that permitted her a daring use of color and luminous flesh tones, and in which she did some of her most sensitive works. One of her art heroes was the eighteenth-century pastelist Quentin de la Tour, best known for his portrayal of Madame de Pompadour. She advised all young artists to study his portraits. She tried her hand at watercolors, drawings, and gouaches.

A striking painting of this period was "Young Women Picking Fruit." Though not an allegory, it was probably suggested by the central panel of her mural. Against a background of grass and flowers, a young woman in a white dress is picking an apple, while a more matronly woman, in dark print dress and hat, sits holding an apple on her lap. Their pose is informal. The scene could be a late summer day in the garden of almost any American country home.

She moved her mother and herself to her own country home, the Château de Beaufresne, in 1893. That it was a huge place for two women alone does not seem to have occurred to her. Compared to the great establishments that both her brothers maintained in America, it was indeed modest.

On the first floor was a circular drawing room; another spacious room, which Mary turned into a studio; a dining room; a kitchen; and a long, glassed-in porch on the garden side, where guests were brought for coffee and conversation after dinner. The second floor had six bedrooms, of which Mary selected the smallest for herself, and two large, old-fashioned bathrooms. The servants' rooms were on the third floor.

Mathilde Vallet still served as Mary's personal maid and housekeeper. She did her hair and helped her dress in the morning. The whole life of this kindly, homely, bespectacled Alsatian woman revolved around her mistress; she seemed to have no private life of her own. The staff also included a cook, a housemaid, a chambermaid, three gar-

"Young Women Picking Fruit," Mary Cassatt. *Courtesy of the Library of Congress.*

deners, and the coachman, Pierre Lefèbre, who would become Mary's first chauffeur.

She ran her large household with the same will to attain perfection with which she approached her painting. Her servants nearly all stayed on with her year after year. To no one, not even her head gardener, did she delegate the authority to cut a rose. She did that herself when she wanted to decorate her table or make a gift to a friend. It was also said that no beggar was ever turned away hungry from her door.

The furniture in the drawing room was Empire style, left there by the De Grasse family. Mary liked it because of its simple lines, though it was not popular at the time and could be bought cheaply. She had some Empire pieces in the bedrooms too, which she painted pea green. The English writer Violet Paget, who wrote under the pseudonym of Vernon Lee, visited Mary in 1895. To a friend she said that she liked the "Louis XVI Château" and the "sort of white bareness of the rooms."

As in her Paris apartment, which Mary Cassatt retained, the real treasures were on the wall—the paintings she had bought because she loved them, not because someone told her they were good, and not to follow a trend but to begin one. To her modern French collection, she gradually added works by earlier artists. One of these was "The Toilet of Venus," by the sixteenth-century Baroque painter Simon Vouet, which she had acquired long before the fad for Baroque art started. She also had some Persian miniatures, and the inner wall of the long porch held a unique collection of nearly a hundred Japanese prints, not all in perfect condition.

Her property covered some forty-five acres, with fruit trees, lawns shaded by giant chestnuts, a vegetable garden where she grew American corn and eggplant, various farm buildings, stables, a carriage house, and a long pool bordered with Lombardy poplars.

Although she could no longer ride, she kept horses and often drove her carriage herself. There were pets, too. She had a parrot named Coco, who occasionally served as a model. Degas wrote a poem about her and her parrot, "To Mademoiselle Cassatt, Apropos of Her Darling Coco" (À Mademoiselle Cassatt, à Propos de Son Coco Chéri). So far as is known, it was the only time she ever received a poem from him, and it was comic rather than sentimental.

She became enamored of the tiny Belgian dogs known as griffons (so called because of a faint resemblance to the legendary griffin). Her first, ordered from a kennel in Brussels, was an elegant creature who arrived with his own raincoat, overcoat, brush, and comb, and even a pocket handkerchief. She named him Napoleon Bonaparte, but called him Nippo. Soon there were others. They were not very popular with her friends, who found them fat, spoiled, noisy, and all too ready to nip at their ankles.

Her mother, whose health had been poor for many years, enjoyed the beauty of the Château de Beaufresne only two years more, when she died at the age of seventy-nine. She remains a nebulous figure in Mary Cassatt's background, the tranquil self-contained model of Mary's "monumentally conceived" portrait "Reading *Le Figaro*," who in her younger days had a reputation of being a scholar, but who as she grew old resigned herself to being the companion of her talented unmarried daughter.

After eighteen years of having a family to look after and to look after her, Mary was on her own. She was now free to do as she wished, travel where and when she wanted, cultivate friends of her choosing. She was fifty-one when she achieved this independence, which she had never sought or demanded—elderly by American standards. The French, more kindly toward women growing old, would have referred to her as "une femme d'un certain âge"—a woman whose age one does not mention. She was as fastidious as ever about her dress. Her tailored outfits were designed by the best Paris dressmakers and she still favored large, elaborate hats. She wore English shoes, since she considered French ones too frivolous. She loved old jewelry; for her lorgnette she wore a long amethyst chain.

The villagers of her neighborhood soon spoke of her as "Notre Mademoiselle," as though she had always lived among them.

II

Impressionists in Later Years

The Eighth Impressionist Exhibition ended the attempts of the Impressionists (or Independents) to stay together in a group. From then on they went their separate ways, meeting only as friends. Among their public, their critics, their old antagonists, their names still remained linked together.

Gustave Caillebotte, the marine engineer and painter whom Manet once referred to as "that quaint millionaire," died in 1893, about the time that Mary Cassatt moved to

Beaufresne. To the French government he left his splendid collection of sixty-five French paintings, with the proviso they be presented in their entirety to the Luxembourg Museum. As a matter of principle Caillebotte had bought the paintings which his colleagues found most difficult to sell elsewhere—in many cases their most original and creative works. The bequest included works of Monet, Pissarro, Renoir, Sisley, Cézanne, Manet, and Degas.

The French government and museum officials regarded this gift with embarrassment and suspicion. In the Académie des Beaux-Arts, there was no less an uproar than had greeted the First Impressionist Exhibition nearly a generation before. Gérôme, who had once voted for Mary Cassatt's admission to the Salon, exploded that if the State accepted such "garbage," it would mean "complete moral distintegration." In spite of the best efforts of Renoir, who was executor of Caillebotte's will, only a little more than half of Caillebotte's legacy reached the Luxembourg. Only Degas had all his works accepted. Of the others, eight Monets, seven Pissarros, two Manets, six Sisleys, six Renoirs, and two Cézannes were deemed worthy of the museum. For Cézanne, it was the first time any of his works had hung in a state museum.

In later years France would find her museums almost bereft of Impressionist art and would blame America and Americans for abducting them. The fate of the Caillebotte legacy is clear proof that her own conservative officials were to blame for the loss.

The irony of the government policy was its inconsistency. Not only Manet, but Monet and Renoir, had already been offered the coveted Legion of Honor award. Renoir had accepted reluctantly, after sending Monet a letter of apology for doing so. Monet, as stubborn as ever, had

"Monet Painting in His Garden," Auguste Renoir. The Bett-mann Archive.

turned down this token recognition. Neither he nor Renoir now had any trouble in selling everything he produced.

Mary Cassatt became better acquainted with these two artists as she, and they, grew older.

Renoir liked her and always gave her large credit for promoting his works and the works of his colleagues in America. She was definitely not a "Renoir woman," the name given to the sensuous, rosy-cheeked models he chose to paint. There were no feminine wiles about her. He could talk with her as easily as with a male companion. Jean Renoir, in his biography, *Renoir, My Father,* relates that once Renoir met Mary Cassatt on a painting tour in Brittany. She carried her easel like a man, he told his son with grudging admiration.

Another time, according to Jean Renoir, they were staying at the same country inn and in the evenings sat and chatted over a jug of cider. One night she said to him with her typical frankness that the one thing against his success was that his technique was too simple, that the public did not like that. Instead of taking offense, he was amused. No need to worry, he told her. The critics could always think up complicated theories later.

Of all the Impressionists, Renoir had had the least troubled life. This was in part due to his easygoing nature. Even in his youth, he could take hardship and hunger in his stride and remain cheerful. Salon rejections depressed him less severely than they did his comrades. Witty and personable, he was accepted as a welcome guest into the home of the wealthy publisher Charpentier, who commissioned a portrait of his wife and children. Renoir did this and other commissioned portraits without qualms. So long as he could go on painting beautiful pictures, he asked for nothing more.

Until he was forty, Renoir lived the carefree life of a bachelor. Then he married Aline Charigot, who had been his model in "Le Déjeuner des Canotiers." Their marriage was extraordinarily happy. His wife was a typical "Renoir woman," beautiful, placid, and feminine. In addition she was a marvelous cook. Their three sons inherited her looks and in their childhood also served as Renoir's models. In 1898 Renoir deserted Paris for good and moved to Cagnes, to a picturesque mansion surrounded by ancient olive trees, with a view of the blue Mediterranean on one side and mountains on the other. Here he was coddled and spoiled by his wife and various women servants and relatives, his every need anticipated. He built a studio amid the olive trees and painted some of his most superb works.

Sorrow eventually caught up with him, as it did with his colleagues. Beginning in 1908 rheumatism confined him to a wheelchair. Four years later he was paralyzed by a stroke and only partially recovered the use of his arms. When World War I broke out, two of his sons, Jean and Pierre, left for the front. Both were severely wounded early in the war. In 1915 his wife died of diabetes.

During those war years, when Mary Cassatt was staying more or less permanently in southern France, she often visited Renoir, sometimes with gifts of American nuts, which her friend Mrs. Havemeyer had been sending her since she turned vegetarian.

Half-paralyzed still, Renoir managed to paint by placing a soft piece of cloth in the palm of his hand and gripping rather than holding his brush in his clawlike fingers. He was feeble and shrunken, but his eyes were as sharp as ever and his wit as irrepressible.

"I adore the brown tones in your shadows," Mary said to him one day. "Do tell me how you do it."

"When you learn to pronounce your r's," Renoir retorted.

The French "r," rolled from deep in the throat, has always been difficult for Anglo-Saxons. Mary had not mastered it in spite of all her years in France.

She also became better friends with Monet in the years after the death of her parents. Monet had never forgotten his wife, Camille, but time had softened the acute pain and guilt caused by her loss, and he had made a new life for himself. In 1883 he took up residence at Giverny, in the southeastern part of his beloved Normandy. He married for the second time—a widow, Madame Hoschède, who was an excellent housekeeper and looked after her own children and Monet's two children by Camille with the same impartial care. They had a charming house bordering the Epte River, with a lovely well-tended garden, where Monet did most of his work. He was now painting "series"—one on windmills, another on poplars, and a third, the most popular of all, on the Rouen Cathedral.

Even the *Figaro* art critic Albert Wolff, so long the ruthless foe of the Impressionists, realized the tide had turned against him and invited Monet to lunch in Paris. Monet ignored the invitation. Except for an annual visit to London, Holland, or Italy, he rarely left Giverny at all. But he always had a warm welcome for his comrades of the days of the Impressionist exhibitions, with whom his ties were as strong as ever.

The Château de Beaufresne was not far from Giverny. Mary Cassatt paid Monet a visit in 1894. Several other friends were visiting him at the same time—Georges Clemenceau, who was writing a book about him; two young journalists and writers, Octave Mirbeau and Gustave Geffroy; and Auguste Rodin, the sculptor. Paul Cézanne was staying nearby at the Giverny inn.

"Rouen Cathedral," Claude Monet. *The Metropolitan Museum of Art, Theodore M. Davis Collection, bequest of Theodore M. Davis, 1915.*

For the past three years Cézanne had been wandering through France, always painting, always alone. At fifty-five he was still almost unknown, except to a few young artists who marveled at his paintings but were too poor to buy them. Though a Cézanne hung on her walls at Beaufresne, Mary Cassatt knew this artist only slightly.

To her friend, Mrs. James Stillman, wife of the American multimillionaire banker, she wrote about him:

> On me, he made the impression of a kind of brigand, with big, red, bulging eyes which gave him a ferocious air . . . and such a violent way of speaking that he literally made the dishes echo. I discovered later that I had let myself be deceived by appearances, for, far from being ferocious, he has the gentlest possible temperament, like a child. . . .

She noted also that he did not look so much like a wild man as in the past. His bushy beard, now gray, was trimmed neatly to a point. He was polite even to a "stupid" maid. Whenever he entered the house, he courteously removed the old beret he wore to protect his bald head.

Other recollections of that reunion come from Gustave Geffroy. When Monet introduced Cézanne to the sculptor, Rodin, he was overwhelmed and almost wept. "Monsieur Rodin is not too proud to shake my hand," he murmured. Fairly recently Cézanne had turned Catholic, and Clemenceau, who was an agnostic, could not resist baiting him about his new faith. Cézanne did not attempt to defend himself. He only looked unhappy.

Of the Impressionist group, Cézanne was the most solitary and sensitive. When he had first come to Paris, Pissarro had sensed his great talent and had instructed him in Impressionist techniques. Cézanne experimented with them briefly and even set himself the task of copying exactly Pissarro's landscapes. Then he abandoned Impressionism to seek his own way, to create from his unique vision paintings that in fact resembled those of the Impressionists no more than they did the smooth and pretty works favored by the Salon jury. His uncompromising nature made it impossible for him to seek favors from highly placed persons who might have sponsored him. After his childhood comrade Émile Zola, unwittingly perhaps, exposed him to ridicule in *L'Oeuvre,* he became more aloof than ever.

Yet he never had the financial worries that afflicted most of the others. His wealthy father provided him with enough money for his modest needs, and when he died left Cézanne a large fortune. For years he was convinced no woman would look at him, but he finally formed an alliance with a model named Hortense, whom he married after his father's death. In spite of some estrangements, theirs was not an unhappy relationship. He had a son, also named Paul, whom he adored. But his real world was in his art, and there no one could enter but himself.

Not long after Mary Cassatt was at Giverny, Monet gave a small dinner for Cézanne, to which he invited Renoir and Alfred Sisley. As they sat down to eat, Monet told Cézanne how happy they were to be able to tell him how fond they were of him and how much they admired his work. Cézanne's eyes filled with tears.

"Ah, Monet, even you make fun of me," he said, and rose and left the room before anyone could stop him. He left the Giverny inn the same day, without troubling to collect his canvases, which Monet arranged to be packed and forwarded to his home at Aix.

Cézanne was even then on the verge of fame and glory that would eclipse them all. An art dealer named Ambroise Vollard, who opened his first shop in Paris in 1894, played an important role in this belated recognition. Vollard had been brought up on the far island of Réunion in the Indian Ocean. He was a swarthy-skinned young man, who spoke softly and slowly and preferred asking questions to giving opinions.

Like Paul Durand-Ruel and George Petit before him, he realized that Impressionist art was a worthwhile investment. He made friends with all the independent artists, but it struck him that what he most needed at the outset of his career was a truly great painter who was unknown and unappreciated. It was Pissarro who first showed him the canvases of Cézanne. Vollard knew at once that this was the man he had been seeking.

He began ferreting out every Cézanne he could locate. The artist was then working at Fontainebleau. Vollard paid him a visit and bought everything in his studio. He took a trip to Aix-en-Provence on a treasure hunt for paintings Cézanne had discarded or given to townspeople, who had stored them away in their attics and barns.

Cézanne's first one-man show, which Vollard opened in November 1895, was a sensation. Cézanne was hailed as "the new master of still life," as "one of the finest, greatest personalities of our time," as "a mysterious man from Provence," who had "suddenly been discovered to be great."

Mary Cassatt could not have been surprised. Since she had first cast her lot with the rebel artists, she had seen her faith in them confirmed, one after another. Of all their group, Pissarro, who had sponsored Cézanne originally, was perhaps the most pleased of all.

This seemingly unattainable success did change Cézanne, but only to the extent it made him rather more gracious and less gruff. He returned to his native Aix, where he built a substantial house just outside of town. Hortense, his wife, disliked rural life and spent most of her time in Paris with their son. Her husband kept to his solitary habits and whenever possible avoided the journalists and miscellaneous curiosity-seekers who descended on Aix in the hope of an interview with the great man, or at least a glimpse of him.

To Émile Bernard, one of his disciples, he remarked, "Talking about art is useless." Every day he went out alone in the countryside to paint the rocks and mountains of the region he loved best. His later works were marked by increasing lyricism. One day in October 1906 he went out as usual, ignoring the suffocating heat and a threatening storm. Intent on his work, he hardly noticed when rain began to fall in huge drops. When he finally had to quit painting, he was soaked to the bones and shivering. On his way back he fell unconscious. A neighbor found him and brought him home. His old housekeeper telegraphed Hortense in Paris, but she and young Paul arrived too late. Cézanne died alone, as he had lived.

There were two of the Impressionists who would never live to know the heady triumphs of fame and success.

One of them was Camille Pissarro, patriarch of the Impressionists and Mary Cassatt's loyal friend and admirer, whom they all turned to in trouble and in doubt. "Everyone copied him, but denied him," Paul Gauguin said of him once. While Monet and Renoir were selling everything they painted at substantial prices, Pissarro was still struggling to support his family on the most modest and uncertain of sales. With all his hardships, he remained serene, placid, benevolent, and intensely interested in the world around him.

Because of an eye ailment, it became impossible for him to paint outdoors in bright sunlight. In his last ten years he returned to Paris and from his windows painted vistas of boulevards with a range of light effects that have never been equaled. He died in 1903, at the age of seventy-three, of blood poisoning caused by an abscess that a homeopathic physician had vainly tried to cure without an operation. Mary Cassatt, who would never admit to sentimentality, wrote a friend in Philadelphia: "Poor Pissarro has just fallen victim to a mistaken diagnosis."

Five months later Durand-Ruel held a Pissarro exhibition in honor of the man who had given so much to so many younger artists, often to the detriment of his own work. His paintings brought from 10,000 to 20,000 francs, far in excess of anything he had earned during his lifetime.

Of all the painters who defied the criteria of the Salon jury, it was perhaps Alfred Sisley, one of the four original Impressionists, whom fate treated the most unkindly. Mary Cassatt did not know him well, if at all, but she loved his art. In extreme poverty from the time his family lost their fortune during the Franco-Prussian War, he fought against heavy odds to support his adored wife and children. His reticent nature made it difficult for him to confess his troubles even to his former comrades.

In 1882 he moved from the Paris suburbs to the ancient town of Moret, in the Forest of Fontainebleau, where in happier days he had painted with Renoir, Monet, and Bazille. He sent works to the Impressionist exhibitions on several occasions but seldom put in a personal appearance. For years his canvases were bought up for twenty-five or thirty francs, less than even Cézanne and Pissarro received in their worst periods. He went through the agony of seeing his wife die of cancer and of being unable to do anything to relieve her suffering.

In all his long years of isolation he continued painting

constantly, especially winter scenes. These were done with great delicacy and have an almost fairylike enchantment about them. The critic Raymond Charmet described him as "the most subtle landscapist of the Impressionist school." Less enthusiastic critics claim he never developed as an artist, as Monet did, and that in his later years his work became mannered. He was certainly the least appreciated of the Impressionists.

In 1899, about four years after his reunion at Giverny with Monet, Renoir, and Cézanne, Sisley died of cancer of the throat at the age of sixty. A sale of his paintings was held a year after his death. At the sale, the French collector Count Camondo paid 43,000 francs for his "The Floods of Port Marly," which now hangs in the Louvre. In a preface to the catalog, Arsène Alexandre wrote: "Sisley saw successively all the joys of life abandon him, except for the joy of painting, which never left him."

12

A Long and Stormy Friendship

A society painter once invited Edgar Degas to a watercolor exhibition. "You will perhaps find our frames and our carpets rather luxurious," he said with a glance at the worn topcoat Degas always wore. "But then, isn't painting an object of luxury?"

"Perhaps for you," retorted Degas. "For us, painting is a first necessity."

Mary Cassatt, for whom painting was also a "first necessity," never ceased to marvel at the quality of her old friend's genius. A perfectionist, he was always inventing new techniques and could not rest until he had mastered them. A follower of Ingres in the elegance of his lines, in his finest works he went beyond Ingres by subordinating lines to a rhythm of light and shadows in a manner suggestive of the Impressionists, with whom he refused to be classified. When it suited him, he used subdued colors. Especially in his later works, he turned to intense blues, yellows, and reds. There were no inferior Degas works, in Mary Cassatt's thinking. Everything he did was touched with excellence.

As a man, he often exasperated her beyond endurance. With Degas she never knew what to expect. Sometimes he acted toward her in the manner of a person who gives candy to a child, only to grab it away.

One day, when they had not seen each other for a long time, he stopped by the Durand-Ruel gallery, where her painting "Boy Before the Mirror" was on display.

"Where is she?" he demanded of Durand-Ruel. "I must see her at once. This is the greatest picture of the century."

When next they met he talked to her in detail about this work, stressing his great admiration for it. Then he spoiled everything with the sneering comment: "It has all your qualities and all your faults. It is the Infant Jesus with his English nurse."

Degas could "dissolve" her, she confessed to Louisine Havemeyer in a rare moment of truth. He could make her feel, "Oh why try, since nothing can be done about it?" That was the reason she had not asked his opinion when she was working on her Chicago murals. If Degas were in a bad mood, he could be "dreadful," as she put it.

Time and again she decided he was utterly impossible and would stop seeing him. Months might go by. Then he

"Woman Drying Her Foot," Edgar Degas. The Metropolitan Museum of Art, H. O. Havemeyer Collection, bequest of Mrs. H. O. Havemeyer, 1929.

would send her a note about some picture of hers he had seen, or they might meet casually at an exhibition, and their friendship would be renewed where they had left off.

She was not the only person to endure his thrusts. He called a certain Academician "the giant of the pygmies." He accused Renoir of painting with "balls of yarn." At one time or another he antagonized nearly all his colleagues. He did not mean half of it. Once he told Renoir that he had only one real enemy—himself.

He once did a portrait of Manet with his wife, Suzanne, at her piano. Manet did not like the way Suzanne was portrayed and cut off that part of the canvas. Degas, furious, retrieved what was left of the portrait and sent back to Manet a still life Manet had given him. But they soon made up. "Who could stay angry with Manet?" Degas demanded, adding that he would have felt differently if Manet had mutilated an Ingres or a Delacroix. Then he would never have forgiven him.

He seemed to take pleasure in appearing ferocious. "If I didn't treat people as I do," he once confided, "I should not have a moment to myself for working." The targets of his abuse were usually bores, chatterboxes, and the inquisitive, including journalists who expected him to take time from painting to talk about Art with a capital "A." Berthe Morisot found him charming and refused to believe the stories that were told about him.

With Mary Cassatt he could also be the most delightful of companions when he wanted to—serious, perceptive, warm in his enthusiasms, original in his thinking. She may have sensed that he was basically shy and that his bearlike manner was assumed to hide this failing from the world.

To outsiders he always praised her, and there were innumerable people who believed she must be a good artist, if only because Degas said she was.

Ambroise Vollard once saw her at an exhibition with a group of people who were talking about the different Impressionists. One of them turned to her, not recognizing her, and said, "But you are forgetting a foreign painter whom Degas ranks very highly."

"Who is that?" she asked, puzzled.

"Mary Cassatt."

Quite naturally and without false modesty, she shrugged and said, "Oh nonsense." Someone in the group murmured, "She must be jealous."

Unlike most artists, Degas hated to part with anything he had done. Durand-Ruel, who was his agent off and on for thirty years, wrote about him: "When he handed over a canvas, his greatest hope was that it would not be sold, and he would unfailingly run it down if he got the chance. . . . He was perfectly capable of taking back one of his pictures on the pretext of improving it, and we would never see it again."

Mary Cassatt once took her friends the Havemeyers to Degas' studio. They were desperately eager to buy something from him, but she had warned them not to be too hopeful. Degas let them look through a portfolio of drawings, which in itself was a concession. Very few visitors were allowed a glimpse of the treasures in his cluttered studio. Mary was exclaiming at the superb drawing of one of the ballet-dancer sketches and Mrs. Havemeyer was looking at it yearningly, not daring to ask for it, when Degas abruptly pulled out two other drawings, signed them, and presented them to the Havemeyers. From his expression, it was obviously a great sacrifice to him. There was no mention of such a sordid matter as price. Mary had to work this out with him later.

"The Dancing Class," Edgar Degas. The Metropolitan Museum of Art, H. O. Havemeyer Collection, bequest of Mrs. H. O. Havemeyer, 1929.

Yet, for some years, Degas had been dependent on sales for a living, like most of his colleagues. The money he had inherited had gone to help out one of his brothers who was in financial difficulties. This was a matter that he never mentioned and that no friend of his risked bringing up.

His own needs were few. He wore the same clothes year after year. That he still looked distinguished was only because they had originally been of excellent material and cut. His only servant was his faithful housekeeper, Zoë. He lived like a hermit on one meal a day, usually vegetables without butter. When he did sell something, it was often as not so he could buy paintings he liked, by Ingres, Delacroix, and his Impressionist friends, or works by the lesser known, and accordingly lower priced, Italian masters.

With children Degas was at his best. At some social gathering a mother was scolding her small daughter for making mistakes in spelling. She turned to him. "It's very bad to misspell, is it not, Monsieur Degas?"

"Very bad," he agreed solemnly.

Out of the mother's hearing he asked the child, "Which would you prefer—to spell correctly and not have ice cream or to make mistakes and have ice cream?"

"To make mistakes and have ice cream," the child said promptly.

Degas nodded. "So would I."

He genuinely adored children and often held parties to which he invited the young Manets, Renoir's small sons, and other sons and daughters of his friends.

In his later years, the idiosyncrasies of Degas became legendary.

Before accepting an invitation to dinner, he insisted on certain conditions. Dinner must be at seven-thirty sharp, not at a later, more fashionable hour. His host must shut up his cat and no guest must arrive with a dog. Women should not wear perfume nor should there be flowers on the table. "What a horror—all those odors," he told Ambroise Vollard. "And when there are things that smell so good—like toast."

He was a fanatic about how his pictures should be framed and found gold frames the height of poor taste. He spied one of his works in a gold frame at a friend's dinner party. When no one was in sight, he removed the canvas, rolled it up under his arm, and departed—not to return.

For many years he had the obsession that he was going blind. Once, when Mary called on him, he kept his eyes tightly closed during her entire visit, claiming that the light hurt them. At an exhibition he refused to pass judgment on paintings he disliked, on the grounds that he could no longer see clearly. But a few moments later he forgot his alleged handicap and reached in his vest pocket to look at his watch.

The most serious break between Mary Cassatt and Degas came over the Dreyfus Affair.

In 1894 the French War Ministry's Intelligence Bureau found out that military secrets were being leaked to the German embassy in Paris. A document, torn in pieces and rescued from the German embassy wastebasket, gave proof that someone with access to the French Bureau files was involved. Suspicion fell on a modest and capable young officer, Captain Alfred Dreyfus, mainly because he was the only Jewish officer in the Bureau. His fellow officers and superiors, all vehemently anti-Semitic, had long been resentful because a Jew was in their midst.

Although Dreyfus' handwriting and that on the document were dissimilar, he was swiftly tried before a military tribunal, stripped of his military rank, and sentenced to life imprisonment on Devil's Island, a hot and unhealthy stretch of rocks off the South American coast.

During his ordeal evidence mounted that he was innocent, that the document in fact had been written by a Hungarian-born officer, Major Walsin-Esterhazy. He was known to be a gambler, always in need of money. He had made reckless statements about his dislike of the French. Moreover, his handwriting did match that on the document. Military and government officials still refused to consider a new trial. They were already too deeply involved. They had to protect their own.

All France became divided between "Dreyfusards" and "anti-Dreyfusards." The Dreyfus Affair had world reverberations. In its wake were duels, street fighting, battles among members of the French parliament, and a bloody uprising in Algeria.

Georges Clemenceau, who felt that the honor of France was at stake, and who was a friend of justice as well as a friend of the Impressionists, wrote some eight hundred articles in his newspaper *L'Aurore,* demanding the release of Dreyfus. Then, on November 25, 1898, *L'Aurore* published an open letter by Émile Zola—"I Accuse" (J'Accuse)—addressed to Félix Faure, president of the French Republic, summarizing all the evidence brought to light thus far on the innocence of Dreyfus, and naming the people involved in concealing that evidence. As a result, Zola himself was put on trial and had to flee to England to escape imprisonment.

"J'Accuse" was one of the greatest political documents of modern times. Largely because of the public furor it aroused, Dreyfus was brought back from Devil's Island. It redeemed Zola in the eyes of the Impressionists, who had turned against him because of his novel *L'Oeuvre.*

Mary Cassatt became a passionate supporter of Dreyfus.

Her own family and many of her American friends were not above occasional slurs against Jewish people. She herself sometimes used the word "Jew" in a derogatory sense. To her this was not the question. It was a simple matter of right and wrong.

Almost alone among his artist colleagues, Degas was an anti-Dreyfusard. He was admittedly anti-Jewish, though his prejudice did not extend to Pissarro. More significant was his conservatism in politics. As the son of a banker and an aristocrat, he had been born and bred in a society that abided by the dicta of the rich and powerful. Though he scorned some things about that society, he was still part of it. If the high echelons of the government and military said Dreyfus was guilty, that settled it.

He went to such an extreme that he sent his housekeeper Zoë to find out whether a certain visitor was for or against Dreyfus before he would see him. He once allegedly dismissed a model on the grounds that she was a Protestant, "and the Protestants are with the Jews behind Dreyfus." Another time he quipped, "That man has a good face; he can't be a Dreyfusard."

Mary found his attitude utterly repulsive and could not abide him during this period. At Pissarro's funeral, which took place at the height of the Dreyfus fracas, she was overheard shouting at Degas, "You're mean to your brother. You're beastly to your sister. You're bad, you're bad!"

Degas remained unaffected by her wrath. At the time she was so angry with him, Ambroise Vollard, who very much wanted Degas as a client, put on exhibition her "Le Salon Bleu," which someone had told him was one of Degas' favorites. The bait worked. Degas walked into Vollard's gallery and stopped before this painting of the daughter of one of his friends, on which he had helped

Mary Cassatt during the springtime of their friendship.

"How talented she is!" he said, and then spoke nostalgically to Vollard of the days when he and Mary had worked so closely together trying to get underway the ill-fated review *Le Jour et La Nuit*.

But the Dreyfus Affair remained a bone of contention between them until 1906, when Dreyfus was at last cleared of all charges against him and restored to his military rank. In time, because the fact that Degas was a great artist loomed larger to Mary than anything else, she forgave and forgot, as she had done so many times before.

13

Trip Back to America

In 1898 Mary Cassatt made her first visit to America since before the Franco-Prussian War nearly thirty years before. Her dread of seasickness was one reason she had postponed it so long. She may also have been afraid that she would no longer feel comfortable in her own country, that she no longer belonged.

"Everyone has two countries, his own and France," wrote her friend Georges Clemenceau, who had begun one of his articles about Dreyfus by explaining the spell which France casts over visitors from foreign lands. Mary Cassatt was the exception. She might live in France but she had remained a one-country person, and that country was the United States of America.

Yet she could not help feeling that America had let her down. Her deepest wish was for recognition at home as an artist of note. One solidly favorable review in America meant more to her than the most ecstatic praise of the French critics. It was not enough for her to be appreciated by "foreigners." She wanted her own people to be aware of who she was. That awareness came with painful slowness.

Back in 1876, two years after her first acceptance by the Paris Salon, the Pennsylvania Academy of the Fine Arts had exhibited several of her paintings. So far as is known, they were the first so-called Impressionist pictures ever shown in America. The Academy displayed a few of her works again in 1878 and 1879, but still showed no inclination to buy anything from their star woman student for their permanent collection.

The National Academy of Design in New York exhibited a portrait she had done of Mrs. W. B. Birny in 1878. That same year the Boston Thirteenth Exhibition of the Department of Fine Arts of the Massachusetts Charitable Mechanics Association—a long and imposing title for what was not really a very important art organization—displayed two of her paintings and a sketch. This resulted in several pleasant notices in Boston papers, and caused a Boston art dealer to ask to act as her agent in that city.

The first serious attempt to appraise her work seems to have been an article by William C. Brownell, which appeared in 1881 in *The Young Painters of America*. This was so filled with inaccuracies, it could hardly have pleased her. It was regrettable that Mary Cassatt had kept her countrymen in comparative ignorance of the work she was doing, Mr. Brownell wrote—as though it were her fault no one knew who she was. After speaking of the "intelligent directness" of her touch, he cited her paintings as a good example of "the better sort of impressionism." And he attributed her success to her apprenticeship at the Pennsylvania Academy, and the fact that she had already acquired her power of expression before "going over" to Edgar Degas!

Her American friends, mostly rich, who stopped to see her on their trips abroad, certainly sang her praises to their rich friends when they went home. Some Americans bought her paintings. But American museums were slow to follow their example, nor was she offered any awards or honors or prizes—any sign that American art societies considered her work worthy of special attention. It could only have been with mixed emotions that she stepped on American shores after her long absence, unsure of what she would find, unsure of how she would be regarded.

There had been many changes. She would have noted that. There were more buildings, more factories, more hustle and bustle. Huge industries were springing up. People were making money hand over foot, that is, if they were ruthless, clever, and not too scrupulous. Poverty had made its appearance, too, to an extent unknown in early America. The word "sweatshop" was applied to the starvation wages and foul working conditions in city ghettos. A journalist and photographer named Jacob Riis was recording for posterity the misery of New York City tenements.

William McKinley was in the White House. American soldiers were fighting Spanish soldiers in Cuba. William Randolph Hearst, whose inflammatory stories in the New York *Journal* were largely responsible for America's involvement in the Spanish-American War, was telling

American people to "Remember the *Maine*." Frederic Remington, a fellow artist Mary Cassatt never met, was in Cuba for Hearst making sketches of the gory combat. His painting of Teddy Roosevelt and his volunteer Rough Riders on San Juan Hill would help Theodore Roosevelt in his campaign to become governor of New York. The use of a painting as political propaganda must have disgusted Mary Cassatt. It may have been one of the reasons why, when Roosevelt became president, she added his name to an increasing list of people she could not abide.

Her brother Alexander had just been appointed president of the Pennsylvania Railroad, following his pleasant years of retirement. In this position, he was one of the most powerful men in industrial America. Mary Cassatt was given an inkling of how paltry her own achievements were judged in comparison by a note that appeared in the Philadelphia *Ledger,* announcing her arrival:

"Mary Cassatt, sister of Mr. Cassatt, president of the Pennsylvania Railroad, returned from Europe yesterday. She has been studying painting in France and owns the smallest Pekingese dog in the world."

The "Pekingese" must have been one of her adored Belgian griffons.

There is no evidence that Philadelphia honored this tall, distinguished woman of "a certain age" as a celebrity or gave her any warmer welcome than was normally due a sister of Alexander Cassatt. She stayed in the town house of the Gardner Cassatts, where she painted pastels of Gardner, Jr., and his little sister, Ellen Mary. Dutifully she paid visits to other Philadelphia relatives. A cousin proudly showed her a painting allegedly by the French painter Nicolas Poussin, but Mary scoffed and said it was a fake. It is unlikely that her astuteness added to her popularity with her cousin.

In the fall she agreed to go to Boston to do portraits of the children of Mrs. Gardiner Green Hammond. Since it had always been against her principles to accept portrait commissions, it is hard to understand why she consented, unless she was bored in Philadelphia. Mrs. Hammond had heard of her skill in portraying children through John Singer Sargent.

Mary Cassatt had met Sargent as a young art student in Paris. At one time she had invited him to join the Impressionists, but he was not interested. Later she refused to see him on the grounds that he had done a "dreadful" portrait of Alexander. When the Hammonds asked her opinion about his work, she dismissed him as a man who wanted "fame and great reputation." Since she was there on Sargent's recommendation, her comment might have been considered poor taste.

The Hammonds gave a series of dinner parties for her in Boston. She took them as an opportunity to talk at length about the Impressionists, whom she called "our little band of Independents," and to urge the guests to collect French art. She also visited the art collection of the Boston Museum, which she summed up as "a disgrace to the Directors." There is no record of how the Bostonians reacted to that.

Actually, her criticism was constructive and true, but could have been applied with equal justice to almost any of the museums in America's big cities. Most of them were still in an embryo state. Few great paintings had reached American shores, and most of those belonged to private collectors. Museums were almost as barren of good European art as when Mary Cassatt had first studied at the Philadelphia Academy.

Her visit to the Boston Museum certainly reinforced her yearning to try and improve the quality of American museums in general—this became one of her dominant concerns in later years.

By March 1899, she was in Naugatuck, Connecticut, staying with the wealthy Whittemore family. Again she had agreed to do portraits, but with no qualms, since the Whittemores were old friends whom she had known in Paris. In all she did three portraits for them. One was of Mrs. Harris Whittemore and her daughter Helen. Another, of Harris Whittemore, Jr., was called "Boy with the Golden Curls." The third and most outstanding was of the matriarch of the family, Mrs. John Howard Whittemore, a pastel with grey tones that she called "Portrait of a Grand Old Lady." Her stay with the Whittemores was probably the pleasantest part of her American visit.

Mary could not have seen much of Alexander while she was in America. Now a stern and imposing grey-haired man with a heavy mustache, he was busy getting the Pennsylvania Railroad back on its feet—by buying up millions of dollars' worth of stocks of rival railroads in the name of the Pennsylvania. The purpose of this, he might have explained to his sister at some time or other, was to call a halt to the disastrous price war among railroad competitors.

Men who depended on the railroads to transport their produce, seeing shipping costs mounting, did not applaud his activities. Farmers of Kansas had already invented the name "Robber Barons" for the masters of the railway systems. In time, the term would be applied to all industrial tycoons who saw the forming of monopolies as an excellent way to increase their profits. In time, laws would be passed to regulate such monopolies. As yet there were no government controls over big business. Under Alexander Cassatt's leadership, the Pennsylvania Railroad prospered as never before.

While Mary prided herself on her knowledge of politics in government—as her father had done—the politics of business was a mystery to her. Alexander and Mary shared a love for horses. They were alike in that both had an indomitable will to succeed in their separate careers. There was a strong bond of affection between them. But she could not understand her brother's passion for making money, nor could he understand her passion for art.

It probably took this visit back to America to make Mary realize how little any of her relatives really cared about art. Her own paintings, which she had given them, were all too often hung in inconspicuous corners or relegated to closets and attics. The lovely Impressionist paintings that she had practically forced Alexander to buy fared little better. To her Philadelphia friends and relatives she was simply Alexander's sister who had never married. To her nieces and nephews she was "Aunt Mary who painted"—and who for some strange reason chose to live in France. Even Robert, whom she had hoped to launch on an artistic career, failed her when he decided to become a banker.

In America at the close of the century, it was only money that counted. Hardly anyone bothered about "the finer things of life." Mary Cassatt had a strong sense of the importance of family relationships and never broke with any of her own. But she was hurt, disillusioned, and a little bitter.

By the end of 1900 she was happily back at Beaufresne, where she supervised more renovations, including the installation of an extra bathroom—which, she wrote a Philadelphia friend, brought her nearly up to American standards. She also planted more than a thousand rosebushes. That gave her more pleasure than anything else.

The Alexander Cassatts traveled to Europe later that

year and stayed at Bad Homburg, in Germany. Alexander had not been feeling well. They hoped the mineral waters of this resort town would restore his health. Mary did not see him again. His daughter, Katherine, whom she had painted as a child, died in 1905, just two years after her marriage. Alexander took the loss hard and his own health deteriorated further. He died suddenly at his Philadelphia home three days after Christmas in 1906, at the age of sixty-seven.

Later Mary would write Robert that the paintings in his father's collection must be worth at least $200,000— hundreds of times what Alexander had paid for them. It was almost pathetic that she felt obliged to put a monetary value on the pictures she had so wanted her brother to love as she did.

During the last years of his life Alexander was working on a mammoth project to extend the Pennsylvania rail lines into New York City through tunnels under the Hudson River. At that time Pennsylvania passengers had to leave the train on the New Jersey side, cross the river on a ferryboat to a Manhattan shore station, and make their way to their destination as best they could.

The tunnels were not yet completed when he died, but plans had progressed far enough so that the work could be done without him. The impressive Pennsylvania Station in New York City opened for the use of both Pennsylvania and Long Island trains in 1910. A statue of Alexander J. Cassatt was unveiled at the dedication ceremony, inscribed to the man "whose foresight, courage, and ability achieved the extension of the Pennsylvania Railroad System into New York City."

A photograph of the statue was sent to Mary. She commented tartly that it looked like him—which was more than one could expect.

14

The Havemeyer Art Collection

When Louisine Elder married the wealthy sugar magnate Henry Osborne Havemeyer in 1883, Mary Cassatt sent them two landscapes, one by Corot and the other by Narcisse Virgile Diaz, another of the Barbizon School of painters. It was her fond hope that Mr. Havemeyer would learn to like art as much as his wife did.

Her friendship with Louisine Elder Havemeyer began when Louisine was a young student in Paris; it lasted half a century. There is no doubt that Mary thought of Louis-

184

ine as her closest woman friend. She had much more in common with her than with her two sisters-in-law, her nieces, the women her nephews married, or with any of her other American women friends and relatives. She was on more intimate terms with her than with her fellow artist Berthe Morisot—probably the only Frenchwoman Mary was genuinely fond of.

In appearance Louisine Havemeyer was rather plain, with irregular features, dark hair, and heavy eyebrows. Her best feature was her eyes, which were large and expressive. Her clothes were expensive but unostentatious, and her manner was simple and unassuming. She was naive rather than sophisticated.

Mrs. Havemeyer was not an artist herself and did not pretend to be creative. That she became a person of excellent taste in art was largely due to Mary Cassatt's guidance. Mary taught her why one painting is good or great and another merely mediocre, how not to be seduced by mere prettiness but to look for strength, line, design, color. Except for this training, Louisine Havemeyer might have been simply another rich woman with more money than she knew what to do with. Step by step, Mary turned her into a collector of art, one of the most fascinating pursuits in the world.

Before his marriage, Henry Havemeyer's interests were limited to business, in which he was as shrewd and ruthless as anyone. By consolidating seventeen sugar refineries into the American Sugar Refining Company, he eliminated all competition. With opposition conquered he was in a position to raise the price of sugar, doing it so gradually and quietly no one thought to complain. "Who cares for a quarter of a cent a pound?" he pointed out.

All the millions he had made by such devices gave him little satisfaction, mainly because by nature he was exceed-

ingly thrifty. He hated to buy a new suit as long as an old
one would still serve. He preferred taking streetcars or
hired hacks to riding in his own carriage. He must have
enjoyed making money but had found no pleasure in
spending it.

From the beginning of his acquaintance with Mary Cassatt he was curiously humble toward this forthright spinster friend of his wife. He was humble about art, too, and
willing to learn. When she began urging him to buy art,
she did not pursue the argument that it would be a good
investment but instead stressed the glamour of owning
beautiful paintings. Future generations would remember
him not for sugar but for art. The Havemeyers' name
would be touched with the same aura of immortality as
the great artists whose works they had acquired.

With all the goodwill in the world, Havemeyer did not
become a connoisseur overnight. There were times when
his obtuseness distressed both his wife and Mary. His slow
but steady progress is illustrated by his changing attitude
toward the works of Gustave Courbet.

Courbet died in exile in Switzerland in 1877. Like so
many other rebel artists, he received official recognition
only after his death. Mary took Louisine to a large Courbet exhibition in 1881, two years before her marriage to
Havemeyer. As she had done on their first meeting, she
discoursed on the merits of the great Realist—his marvelous execution, his color, and, in Mrs. Havemeyer's words,
"that poignant palpitating medium of truth through
which he sought expression."

They stopped before Courbet's "The Cherry Tree
Branch" (La Branche de Cerisiers), a half-length portrait
of a nude drawing down a cherry branch before her face.
"Did you ever see such flesh painting?" demanded Mary.
"You must have one of his nude half-lengths some day."

After her marriage, Mrs. Havemeyer for a long time tried vainly to interest her husband in Courbet. Only when bullied by both her and Mary Cassatt did he buy his first one, a picture of some cows in a meadow. A year after that Mrs. Havemeyer saw "La Branche de Cerisiers" in Durand-Ruel's New York gallery. Delighted at the coincidence, she asked to have it sent to her home so her husband could look at it. She could tell by his expression he did not approve of it. After a day or so she sent it back.

"I knew you did not really want it," Mr. Havemeyer said.

On the contrary, she told him, she wanted it very much. She thought it one of the loveliest pictures she had ever seen. If they owned it, she would keep it in her closet and not show it to anyone. The next day it was back. Mr. Havemeyer had yielded to her whim. In time he grew to like it as much as she did. Instead of hiding it in a closet, he proudly showed it to all their friends. His wife once heard him say that it was his favorite, next to his Rembrandts.

Over the years the Havemeyers acquired some thirty-five of Courbet's paintings, including "La Femme au Perroquet," a portrait of another lovely nude, with a parrot. Like "La Branche de Cerisiers," it now hangs in the Metropolitan Museum of Art.

When Mr. Havemeyer wanted a painting he usually got it, but there was one time when he failed. At an exhibition in 1891, he stopped short before Courbet's "The Stone Breakers" (Les Casseurs de Pierres), standing before it as in a trance. He did not even hear Mary Cassatt whisper to his wife, "He is bowled over by that Courbet." To his intense disappointment, the owner of the painting refused to sell it at any price. "Les Casseurs de Pierres" finally found a home in the Dresden Museum. It was destroyed by bombardments during the Second World War.

"The Woman with a Parrot," Gustave Courbet. The Metropolitan Museum of Art, H. O. Havemeyer Collection, bequest of Mrs. H. O. Havemeyer, 1929.

Édouard Manet was another painter whom Mrs. Havemeyer and Mary Cassatt taught Havemeyer to appreciate.
Mrs. Havemeyer's interest in Manet was aroused when she
saw a crowd jeering at two of his paintings at a Salon exhibition. One of them was a portrait of the editor, Roche-
fort. "You must not go near it," a disdainful young man
said with a smirk. "Don't you see his face? He's coming
down with smallpox." Trained as she was by Mary Cassatt, she realized that an artist who could provoke such an
outburst was worth investigation.

With Mary's help, she and her husband bought a large
number of Manets. Several were from his early Spanish
period. Another was "Le Bal de L'Opéra," for which they
outbid the French collector Count Camondo. One of Manet's most original works, it shows a crowd of well-dressed
men at the entrance to the Opéra ball. The emphasis is
on their hats—a veritable sea of hats of all imaginable
sorts: "High hats, low hats, black hats, silk hats . . . hats
on straight, hats on crooked," as Mrs. Havemeyer described it.

Mary Cassatt heard indirectly that Georges Clemenceau
was thinking of selling a portrait Manet had done of him.
The Havemeyers happened to be in Paris, so she drove
them out to his villa in the suburbs to see it. The portrait
was an excellent likeness—the same dark hair and dark
eyes beneath shaggy eyebrows—but Clemenceau said he
had never liked it and would be happy to get rid of it.
Then, as if the subject bored him, he began a long discussion with Mary about the proposed separation of the
church and the state in France, a matter in which he, as an
agnostic, was passionately concerned. Only when they had
exhausted the subject did he mention the painting again.
He asked 10,000 francs for it. Mrs. Havemeyer bought it
at once.

With Mary, the Havemeyers also went to see another
Manet portrait, which the dealer called "a wonderful
painting of a very ugly man." The subject was George
Moore, the Irish novelist and amateur artist, who had fre-
quented the same cafés as the Impressionists and who was
an old friend of Mary's. She said she had always considered the portrait one of the finest things Manet had done.
"Of course George Moore did not like it," she added,
"and said horrid things about it to me." (She had once
done an etching of Moore herself and had not tried to
glamorize him either.)

The Havemeyers gave the portrait a place of honor in
their New York home, where it attracted more attention
than any of their other Manets.

Mary also introduced the Havemeyers to Durand-Ruel
and performed the same service for the dealer Ambroise
Vollard, after he had successfully launched Cézanne. "I've
been talking to Mr. Havemeyer about you," she told Vollard one day. "So do put all your best things aside for
him. You know who I mean by Havemeyer?"

Like all Paris dealers, Vollard had done homework on
American millionaires and knew very well that Havemeyer was the Sugar King of the United States. He
awaited his visit anxiously and was distressed when, near
the hour of their appointment, a plainly dressed man got
out of a shabby cab and came into his shop. He did not
want to keep the wealthy American waiting while this un-
prepossessing customer haggled over the price of a minor
engraving. But the stranger promptly asked to see his
Cézannes, bought two of them without quibbling, then
presented his card. He was Mr. Havemeyer. Later the
Havemeyers bought more Cézannes from Vollard, including his "Aqueduc aux Pins Parasols," which the American
fancied because it reminded him of a fresco he had admired in Pompeii.

"George Moore," *Édouard Manet. The Metropolitan Museum of Art, H. O. Havemeyer Collection, bequest of Mrs. H. O. Havemeyer, 1929.*

Understandably, Vollard liked Mary Cassatt not only because she was a good artist but because she had wealthy, art-buying American friends.

"Mary Cassatt!" he wrote in his book, *Recollections of a Picture Dealer.* "At the time of my first attempts, when I used to ask myself anxiously what the morrow would be like, how often did she get me providentially out of a difficulty. . . . It was with a sort of frenzy that generous Mary Cassatt labored for the success of her comrades: Monet, Pissarro, Cézanne, Sisley, and the rest."

Although Mary Cassatt had begun by introducing the Havemeyers to contemporary French art, they later made use of her judgment in buying paintings of what she always called the "Old Masters." In January 1901 the Havemeyers, with Mrs. Havemeyer's sister, Mrs. Peters, met Mary in Genoa for a major art-hunting expedition through Europe.

"In the bright sunlight of the early morning, from the upper deck I could see Miss Cassatt walking impatiently up and down the wharf," Mrs. Havemeyer wrote in *Sixteen to Sixty—Memoirs of a Collector.* Her detailed account of this trip shows how much she and her husband valued Mary Cassatt as a guide and companion in their travels.

In Genoa they stayed long enough to see some paintings by the Flemish artist Anthony Vandyke. They went on to Turin, where in spite of bitter cold they went out to admire the Egyptian "Black Rameses," dating back to 1400 B.C. In Milan, equally frigid, they looked at works by the Renaissance artists Luini, Veronese, and Moroni. Mr. Havemeyer was ready to buy one of the Moronis from a local dealer until Mary discouraged him, saying it was not up to the artist's usual standard.

With relief they traveled south to Naples and crossed

the Strait of Messina to Taormina in warm Sicily, where the Greek colonists had built a lovely theater. Mary, who adored Greek art, brought up for discussion a theory of the French encyclopedist Denis Diderot that the modern world would still be producing works worthy of the Greeks, had not Christianity, with its draped angels and martyred saints, intervened. Diderot's theory was certainly no less controversial than it had been more than a century before, when the many volumes of his enlightened encyclopedia were twice suspended from publication by royal decree. At least it probably provided the Havemeyers and Mrs. Peters with a lively subject of conversation.

They continued their travels through Sicily. Syracuse displeased them because of the dirt. They were thrilled with the Greek temples at Girgenti, although the danger of bandits made it necessary for them to travel with armed guards. In Palermo Mary produced a copy of *La Grande Grèce,* a book about Greece by the French archaeologist François Lenormant. It was the last word on travel and had inspired George Gissing's *By the Ionian Sea,* she told her friends. They must read it.

After re-crossing the Strait of Messina, they spent a day in Reggio in southern Italy, where Mary and Mrs. Havemeyer did some shopping for antiques. They were sightseeing in Rome some days later. Mary took her friends to see the portrait of Pope Innocent X by the Spaniard Velásquez, which she discovered no longer impressed her as it had done in her youth. Mr. Havemeyer expressed the wish to buy a Velásquez, and Mary sent off a note to Durand-Ruel to see what he could do. Dealers in Rome really had nothing interesting to show them.

In Bologna Mary searched out the works of a Renaissance artist who had been a native of that city— Domenichino. Domenichino was an artist whom Degas ad-

mired greatly, she told her friends. It was a pity he was
not better known. She did not tell them—and she probably did not admit to herself—that this trip was more or
less a pilgrimage for her, not only a return to the days
when she had studied in Rome and Parma, but a visit to
the Italy Degas had come to love when he was still a very
young man.

They went next to Ravenna, which is rich in Byzantine
mosaics. The style, such a contrast to Classical forms,
caused Mary to reflect on the beginning of art. Did it orig-
inate in Egypt, Persia, or along China's Yangtze River?
Could caravans have carried examples of the carved patterns of Chinese fret to Greece? The conundrum could
have occupied her and her friends for an evening of sur-
mise.

In lovely Venice they visited the Basilica of San Marco
and the Ducal Palace, and admired the paintings of the
fifteenth-century Venetian, Vittore Carpaccio. They went
to Padua to marvel at the sculptures of Donatello, who
Mary said had absorbed the best of Classical art and com-
bined it with a touch of the Renaissance.

In the fabulous city of Florence, they engaged a scout
named Arturo Harmisch, whom Mary Cassatt had met
when she was in Italy before. He and his wife took them
to an out-of-the-way palace, where, in a dimly lit room,
hung a portrait which Veronese had done of his wife.
Mary Cassatt sensed at once that it had great quality.
When the Havemeyers seemed uncertain, she convinced
them to buy it by threatening to sell something of her
own and get it for herself. Some of Harmisch's so-called
finds proved of dubious value, but the Havemeyers did
get several other paintings through him, including a fine
Madonna by the fifteenth-century Florentine, Filippo
Lippi.

Mrs. Peters had had enough of train trips and traipsing through museums by now. They took her to Paris, and after she was comfortably installed in Mary Cassatt's apartment, the other three went on to Madrid.

In the Prado, Mary showed the Havemeyers their first El Greco. Born in Crete, this sixteenth-century painter had acquired the name of "the Greek" in Spain, where he passed most of his life. Outside of Spain he was still very little known. Very excited, Mr. Havemeyer announced he must have something by this stunning painter. Mary Cassatt said she would try to find him what he wanted. A little later they were passing an art shop when she stopped short.

"There he is!" she cried, pointing to a small painting in the window. "That is a Greco, or I am mistaken, and a fine one. . . . No one else could have done those hands."

She was right. The painting was El Greco's "Christ Bearing the Cross." The Havemeyers bought it from the Spanish art dealer for the pittance of $250.

Mary Cassatt wanted her friends to own something by Goya. On her advice they bought his "Portrait of Wellington" for $4,000 and his two Sureda portraits for less than $10,000. After that purchase, the Havemeyers took an excursion to southern Spain, but Mary Cassatt stayed on in Madrid to see what else she could line up for them.

By the time they returned she had unearthed some truly remarkable offerings—another Goya, "Majas on the Balcony," and three more El Grecos. One of these was his landscape "View of Toledo," which the art collector Henri-Pierre Roche would call "a picture which possesses me to such a degree that I feel I possess it." The other two were "Assumption of the Virgin" and "Cardinal Guevara." Mr. Havemeyer first objected to the red-robed cardinal because he was wearing spectacles, but later agreed

this was unimportant. Eventually the Havemeyers purchased all four paintings.

The "Assumption of the Virgin" measured fifteen feet
across, and Mrs. Havemeyer had to admit it was too large
to show in their New York home. She offered it to the
Metropolitan for the purchase price of $17,000, but the
museum refused it. Mary Cassatt then wrote the Art Institute of Chicago about it. That is where it now hangs. This
was one time when she could, by direct action, redeem the
promise she had made to herself in Boston to improve the
quality of art in American museums.

While Mary Cassatt and her friends were still in Madrid, they heard that a certain Marquis de Heredias was offering for sale a painting by Goya called "Bella Librera."
They went to see it, but Mary would not let the Havemeyers buy it. She did not think it was genuine. Some
years later they saw the real "Bella Librera" in France,
and promptly purchased it. The incident was one more
proof to the Havemeyers of Mary Cassatt's infallible judgment.

"Miss Cassatt had the 'flair' of an old hunter," Mrs.
Havemeyer wrote later, "and her experience had made
her as patient as Job and as wise as Solomon in art matters."

Other American business tycoons were now buying European art treasures, sometimes by the carload. The
names of J. Pierpont Morgan, Cornelius Vanderbilt, William Whitney, Peter Widener, Henry Frick, stand out.
They did it as an investment, for reasons of vanity, to ease
their consciences, as a solace for their lives of money-grub-
bing, and only occasionally because they loved beauty.

Not all were lucky enough to have a Mary Cassatt to
guide them. There were some costly mistakes. Left to
themselves, their taste was all too often uncertain. They

favored the worst of the French Academicians, the more sentimental the better. They bought monstrosities in the naive belief that because something was old it was valuable. Unscrupulous agents foisted on them canvases turned out by the yard in the Paris studios of indigent artists—of which the only merit was their expensive frames. Of Vanderbilt's entire collection, for which he had paid $1,500,000 by the time of his death in 1885, it was later said there was only one good painting—a Delacroix. The wizard of finance Morgan paid an enormous sum for his first "Raphael," only to learn that it had been offered to all the leading European galleries at a far lower price and rejected as a fake.

Spurred on by their rivals, some of these magnates grew wiser. They hired irreproachable art experts as agents to make their purchases or relied on reputable dealers. They assembled formidable collections.

Mary Cassatt worried, because America had so many private art collectors that Europe would soon be depleted. At the same time, she was appalled at how slow American museums were in acquiring important pictures. For this she blamed the American people. They should have insisted that their galleries buy good things. It was not money but taste that was lacking, she said.

Ironically, it was because of the bequests of the nineteenth-century Robber Barons, not because of public protests, that the American people first began to see great art in their own museums.

The splendid Havemeyer collection was eventually bequeathed to the Metropolitan Museum of Art in New York. It would be an exaggeration to give Mary Cassatt all the credit for it. Durand-Ruel and other dealers had also advised the Havemeyers, and their own judgment became increasingly sound. A modern critic refers to "the exquisiteness of the Havemeyer taste in art." An early curator at the Metropolitan went so far as to say that "the Havemeyer object is recognizable no matter where it turns up."

Mary Cassatt assisted other wealthy Americans in their art purchases—her own brothers, Mrs. Potter Palmer, the Whittemores (whose portraits she did in Naugatuck), Mrs. Montgomery Sears, and the banker James Stillman. But it was the Havemeyers whom she guided over the longest period and with the greatest satisfaction.

15

America Recognizes an Expatriate

The first decade of the 1900's marked several changes in Mary Cassatt's artistic techniques. Because her eyesight was not as keen as before, she used freer brush strokes. Her compositions became more informal and had greater spontaneity and freshness. She became increasingly aware of the infinite variety of movement in her child models. Instead of trying to pose them, she let them take their own poses. One of her mother-and-child portraits shows the mother sewing, while her small daughter stands with her elbows resting on her mother's knees. One child refused all inducements to pose and instead climbed into its mother's arms and fell asleep. Mary did a pastel of them, "Mother Holding a Child Asleep in Her Arms."

At Beaufresne she did much of her painting outdoors, at the edge of her pool. It was a delightful spot on warm September days. A charming painting of this period is "The Bath," now in the Petit Palais in Paris, which shows two women in brightly colored dresses sitting in a boat with their two babies.

Most of her models now were village women and their offspring. This was a radical departure from the upper-class women with well-groomed and well-scrubbed infants she had favored in the past. Once she had made the change, she became enthusiastic. "Most women with nurses do not know how to hold their children," she told a friend with the air of having made a great discovery. What she found in her peasant women was a rhythm of curves—their curved arms as they held their babies, and their curved backs as they bent over their small children.

One of Mary Cassatt's local models, who posed for her when she was sixteen, disclosed later that "Our Mademoiselle" always wore a white blouse while painting, that she was serious but not severe, but that she could be difficult. Neighborhood children liked posing for her, since she gave them books and toys to entertain them, but they were petrified by her ferocious little griffons.

She had become interested in local politics. When elections were coming up she invited her neighbors in and practically ordered them whom to vote for. Several old and wealthy French families who lived in nearby châteaus sought her acquaintance.

Once she took her nieces to tea at the Château Villotran, owned by the Mellon family. The tea service was loaded into a donkey cart, which was trundled along through the wide gardens to a pagoda known as "The Temple of Love." Two uniformed footmen then served the guests. The little girls never forgot that tea party.

The Gardner Cassatts and their children came to Beaufresne on their frequent vacations abroad. It was a stopping-off place for other American relatives, too, on their trips to Europe. Berthe Morisot came to see Mary there before her death in 1895. From time to time she saw other old French friends: Clemenceau, Mallarmé, George Moore, and Ambroise Vollard.

She had become a vegetarian herself but for her guests she served the finest French cuisine. When she heard of a particularly delectable dish in a Paris restaurant, she sent Mathilde Vallet to get the recipe from the chef. Sometimes her guests fished for trout in her well-stocked pool. They were cooked and served as an entrée before the main repast.

Conversation, nearly always directed and controlled by the hostess, was lively. To art, literature, politics, and philosophy she added a new interest, spiritualism, which was all the rage in the 1900's. The scientist Sir Oliver Lodge, the psychologist and writer William James, the American diplomat Poultney Bigelow, and other notables were attending séances of the medium Madame de Thèbes in the Paris home of Mary's friend Mrs. Montgomery Sears. In a letter to Mrs. Havemeyer's daughter, Electra, Mary described a séance she attended, held by another friend, Mrs. Schelling, at which a table had risen four feet off the floor *twice*. She theorized that the religion of the Egyptians and Greeks might have been founded on such happenings, which were now being rediscovered "through a scientific road."

The Havemeyers gave Mary a Renault limousine in

1906, as a token of their appreciation. Old-fashioned in many ways, she had postponed the purchase of a car. Once she had one, she found she adored motoring. Pierre Lefèbre, her coachman, took driving lessons so he could act as her chauffeur. The Renault served her nearly twenty years, until her death. She traveled all over Europe in it.

If she wanted to go to Paris for a few days to attend an art exhibition or some other cultural event, she still had her apartment on the rue de Marignan.

Because winters were cold at Beaufresne, as in Paris, she rented the Villa Angeletto, near the town of Grasse in southern France, as a winter home. Famous for its manufacture of perfume, Grasse was set amidst huge plantations of tuberoses, lavender, lilies of the valley, and carnations. Centuries before, it had been part of the feudal estate of the De Grasse family, from whose descendants Mary Cassatt had purchased Beaufresne. She considered Villa Angeletto a mere cottage, but it had ample space for her servants, her dogs, and her occasional visitors.

With her varied surroundings, her travels, her many friends, and her work, her life was very full and stimulating. She had a freedom and independence that she could hardly have found in America under any circumstances. It may well have been that the recognition at home she once craved so desperately now seemed less urgent, less vital.

Yet almost imperceptibly her reputation was spreading in America. Her paintings were appearing with increasing regularity in exhibitions across the country, in part due to the efforts of Paul Durand-Ruel, who was submitting them without even bothering to tell her.

She perhaps first became aware of what was happening in the spring of 1904, when Harrison Morris, managing director of the Pennsylvania Academy of the Fine Arts, wrote her that she had been awarded the Walter Lippincott Prize of $300 for her painting "Caress," submitted by Durand-Ruel without her knowledge to the Academy's seventy-third Annual Exhibition. It made the Academy most happy that the painting should receive this award, Morris said, "as denoting an honor paid to a distinguished artist who is also our townswoman."

She declined the prize from her alma mater. It must have given her some satisfaction to do so. Her long and polite letter to Mr. Morris, larded with expressions of gratitude, explained that it was against her principles to accept. Since the first exhibition of the Independents (actually the fifth, but the first in which she had participated), she had followed the example of her colleagues in avoiding juries, medals, and awards. "Surely no profession is so enslaved as ours," she concluded. The directors of the Academy apparently did not think she meant what she said, for later in the summer they asked her to serve as a juror for another exhibition. Again she refused, for the same reasons.

That October, four Mary Cassatt paintings, including "The Caress" (Caresse Enfantine), were shown at the Seventeenth Annual Exhibition of the Art Institute of Chicago—the first time she had been so honored. "Caress" was awarded another prize, in the amount of $500. Once more she refused it. To the Art Institute's director she wrote requesting that the prize money go to some young artist or student who needed it. In accordance with her wishes, it was given to Alan Philbrick, a graduate of the Art Institute school, who was already in Paris on a fellowship.

Young Philbrick visited her at her Paris apartment to thank her. She impressed him as a "fiery and peppery lady," and he admitted he was scared to death of her. Rich and well established, she seemed in a different world from him and his fellow art students, who were living a nearly penniless existence, with no thought of the morrow.

Near the end of 1904 the French government presented her with the Legion of Honor, the coveted award that Renoir had accepted with misgivings and Monet had rejected, and that very rarely was offered to a foreigner, especially a woman. Her friend Georges Clemenceau, who two years later would become prime minister of France, growled at her that he did not need to see her new ribbon to know she was a great painter.

The *American Art News* reported her winning of the Legion of Honor and commented that it was not surprising, since the French "Minister of Fine Arts and the Director of Fine Arts, Mr. Marcel, are both enthusiastic admirers of Miss Cassatt's work." Certainly the award impressed American art circles more than any of the other tokens of esteem that France had yet offered her.

Mary Cassatt's only recorded reaction is in a letter she sent to a young protégé, the Philadelphia artist Carroll Tyson. Her one hope, she wrote, was now that she had the "ribbon" American museum directors would pay her more attention when she urged them to acquire "Old Masters."

The American colony in Paris, who had ignored her work year after year, appointed her honorary president of the Art League in that city, which ran a hostel for American art students. In this capacity, she gave short talks on art to the students, in a simple and direct manner that was an inspiration to them. To two "deserving students" she presented scholarships, with the provision that they should spend a year in Saint-Quentin, on the Somme River, to study the seventeenth and eighteenth century pastelists who had influenced her own work.

A new Pennsylvania state capitol was built at Harrisburg in 1905. The state sponsored a mural competition, for which Mary Cassatt submitted two paintings of mothers and children. When she heard that the project was rife with graft and that unscrupulous politicians were pocketing a high percentage of the large sums involved, she withdrew her submissions. It was typical of her upright character that she would have nothing to do with an enterprise tinged with corruption, even though it might have been to her personal advantage to do so.

The loss of her brother Alexander the following year was such a shock she fell seriously ill. She would never be really well again. Henry Havemeyer died almost a year later, in December 1907. This was another blow to Mary, who had helped transform the American sugar magnate into a person who could judge a Cézanne and appreciate a Courbet. Mrs. Havemeyer urged her to come stay with her in New York during this hard period of her loneliness. Because of her own uncertain health, she postponed going until the fall of 1908. As always, the crossing made her violently seasick. She had to be carried off the ship to Mrs. Havemeyer's home on Sixty-sixth Street and Fifth Avenue.

This was the first time she had seen the mansion that housed the Havemeyers' great art treasures, and where they had lived since 1889. Inspired by the Byzantine architecture in Ravenna, the decorators had designed a mosaic hall and ten mosaic pillars at the entrance to the art gallery. There was also a Rembrandt room, where guests were invited on Sunday afternoons to listen to chamber music while they looked at the world's greatest paintings.

Over the years the guests had included many American celebrities, among them the architect Stanford White, the sculptors Augustus Saint-Gaudens and William Mac-Monnies, and the editor Richard Watson Gilder. Mrs.

Theodore Roosevelt—whose husband Mary Cassatt could not stand even though he was president of the United States—arrived one day almost without warning, for a look at the most important art collection in America. She made the rounds of the gallery without comment and left without thanking her hostess. The favorite guest of the Havemeyers was always Helen Keller. It astounded them that this remarkable woman, who was both deaf and blind, could distinguish between Mrs. Havemeyer and her sister, Mrs. Peters, merely by touching their hands.

In the atmosphere of this luxurious home, the setting for the many beautiful paintings she had persuaded the Havemeyers to buy, Mary Cassatt recovered slowly from the ordeal of the Atlantic crossing. For several weeks she could hardly leave her bed. She vowed that this would be her last trip to America, which it proved to be.

By Christmas she was well enough to go to Philadelphia and spend the holidays with the Gardner Cassatts. A high point of her visit was a dinner party they gave for her, at which an African hunter, Percy Madeira, was present. Mary was so spellbound by his tales of Africa that she refused to leave the table after dinner, when the ladies were all supposed to retire to the drawing room.

Sometime during her stay, her banker brother took her to see his enormous new fifty-three-room country home, near Berwyn, Pennsylvania. Later, she wrote her artist friend Carroll Tyson that if she had to live in America, she would want to stay always in the country. Town houses were so dark and ill-lighted they depressed her.

In 1909, after she had returned to France, she was elected an associate member of the New York National Academy of Design. She refused once more as a matter of principle. She did not want to be known in America as a member of any art academy, any more than she had been willing to serve on art juries or accept prizes. All she sought was to have recognition as an artist of quality.

She presented the Pennsylvania Academy with two Courbet paintings in 1912: "Unknown Lady" and "Mayor of Ornans." She got them through Durand-Ruel with the understanding that he would accept some of her work in exchange. The Academy wrote and thanked her, and then had what she called the "audacity" to add that it had noticed it had nothing of hers, and would she please send something.

"I told them I had been exhibiting for years at the Academy," she said many years later, still burning with indignation, "and they had never asked me my prices, although they had funds for buying contemporary American art."

Two years after this, the Pennsylvania Academy awarded her its Gold Medal of Honor, in appreciation of her "eminent services to the Academy." This she did not refuse. Since the award was given her as an artist, not for any particular painting, and since there was no money involved, she had no scruples about accepting.

16

A Late Romance

Beginning in 1909, a sleek Mercedes limousine, chauf-
feured by a huge, mustached Frenchman, frequently
drove up the curved driveway leading to the Château de
Beaufresne. The single passenger was James Stillman, the
multimillionaire American banker. A handsome man past
middle age with dark hair and shaggy eyebrows, he was
six years younger than Mary Cassatt and one of her staun-
chest and strongest admirers.

She had first met him and his wife in the early 1890's. It

is thought that Alexander Cassatt introduced them. They had expressed interest in buying art, and she had given them advice as she did to her other wealthy American friends. She had been on excellent terms with both of them, especially Mrs. Stillman. Since then Mrs. Stillman had left her husband, reportedly because he was too difficult and demanding.

In his forty years on Wall Street, Stillman had become a giant in American industry. As president of the National City Bank, he had taken part in efforts to manipulate the stock market, at least once to the ruin of numerous small stockholders. He had helped J. P. Morgan and John D. Rockefeller build their financial empires, and thereby profited himself. According to government figures compiled later, Stillman, Morgan, and First National Bank President George F. Baker once controlled a determining share of America's capital, with total resources of more than $3 billion. On his own, in addition to his bank presidency, Stillman had held office in some forty-one companies and subsidiaries.

On Wall Street he was known as "the man in the iron mask," unapproachable and terrifying. Two brokers were once comparing him to the Sphinx. "If the two ever met, I'll wager the Sphinx spoke first," one of them said. Someone else referred to his "cold smile of a Japanese statesman." He took it for granted that everyone who came to see him was after something. In his office his customary greeting was, "Well—and what do *you* want of me?"

Now he lived alone with his many servants in a palatial Paris mansion on the rue Rembrandt, facing the Parc Monceau. In semiretirement, his only connection with his bank was the daily cables of advice he sent across the Atlantic.

He had come to love France with a romantic passion.

"A French servant would rather have a pleasant word than a piece of silver," he once said. "They make a grace of living and value graciousness in others." In order to communicate properly with the French people, he learned the French language flawlessly. He had nothing but contempt for certain retired business associates who used their leisure to gamble in casinos or take water cures at fashionable spas.

His own days were filled. He took walks in the Parc Monceau, browsed in bookstores, attended literary, artistic, and historical conferences, art exhibitions and auctions, concerts, the theater, and the opera. With all his multiple interests, he was essentially a lonely man. Of all the many people he knew, Mary Cassatt was the one he most trusted. She never met the James Stillman of the iron mask. She knew him as a simple, friendly man, a little too passive, sometimes ingenuous.

In her he found qualities lacking in younger and more beautiful women. Her forceful character appealed to him. He was impressed by her success and by the fact that she had achieved the unusual. Moreover, she was the only person he had met who wanted nothing of him. On the contrary, she gave him what he most desired at this stage of his life. She helped him enlarge his cultural perceptions.

Like Henry Havemeyer, like other mighty magnates of American industry, he had found that buying art gave him more satisfaction than anything else. Mary Cassatt taught him to avoid the traps into which his rival collectors fell. She did not want him to be another J. P. Morgan, who in her opinion bought everything that caught his fancy, no matter what the cost.

She once stopped him from buying two heads by the eighteenth-century French painter Jean Baptiste Greuze, because she considered them sentimental. When, on his

Mary Cassatt at Grasse, 1914. From Miss Mary Cassatt: Impressionist from Pennsylvania, *by Frederick A. Sweet. Copyright 1966 by the University of Oklahoma Press.*

own, he bought a painting by Madame Vigée-Lebrun, one of the few women painters before her time to achieve renown, she witheld her approval. She did not care for this contemporary and friend of Marie Antoinette, of whom she said scornfully, "She painted herself." Largely with her help, Stillman amassed a most notable collection of works by Ingres, Murillo, Moroni, Rembrandt, Titian, Fragonard, and other truly great artists.

On occasion she bullied him. One day they went to René Gimpel's gallery to look at a Velasquez. "Buy it," she ordered. "It's shameful to be rich like you. Such a purchase will redeem you." Stillman smiled and obeyed.

Stillman often had Sunday dinners at Beaufresne. When Mary was in Paris, he had tea at her apartment or invited her to dine with him on the rue Rembrandt, in his vast dining room where the red velvet walls were the background for his Titians, and where a footman stood behind each chair. She took such luxury in her stride. After all, she had known rich people all her life.

When she was at Grasse, he sometimes motored down to see her. In the Alpes-Maritimes, where Grasse is located, this captain of American industry became known as "Papa Bonbon," because of his custom of tossing candies from his limousine to village children.

There were times when Mary became angry with him —because he did not share a certain one of her many enthusiasms, because his calm passivity annoyed her, or for some other reason—and would refuse to see him. He bided his time patiently, trying to win back her favor with gifts for her griffons of fancy collars or feeding bowls from Tiffany's. Eventually she would relent and greet him as before at Beaufresne with a smile of welcome.

Her talk about politics frankly bored him. One day she took off on a dissertation on woman suffrage, but he cut her short with a tale about Madame and Monsieur Wildenstein of the Wildenstein Galleries, which held her attention because she was involved.

The Wildensteins had brought him into their private apartment to show him a certain Italian painting, but he had ignored it to stare at a pastel by Mary Cassatt hanging on their walls. When they noticed his interest, they began talking about its charm and beauty, its exquisite colors and masterful drawing. Madame Wildenstein even took it in her hands with such tenderness he thought she was going to kiss it. Feigning indifference, he had asked the price.

"Ah, Monsieur, this is ours, it's not for sale," she told him, and went on to talk more about Mary Cassatt's talent and how much they regretted they had not realized earlier that she was a genius. Subsequently he invited the Wildensteins to his home to see his own collection of Cassatts, which impressed them greatly.

Stillman owned some twenty-four of her paintings and admired her work so much he once predicted that within ten years it would sell for as much as any Degas. She shrieked with laughter. Although she was not ashamed of what she had done, she had no illusions that she compared with the great Degas. She once expressed the wish that Stillman would not give her paintings to a museum. She felt that her pictures were made for private homes, that they were pleasant and easy to take, but "had nothing for the public."

As single people with no responsibilities, both Mary Cassatt and James Stillman traveled a good deal. When they were away they wrote letters to each other. Mary Cassatt's letters to him were warm, friendly, solicitous, and far more interesting than her letters to her own family.

In one letter to Stillman she spoke of a Chardin paint-

ing she had seen in Paris. She had spent "an instructive
half-hour" studying it, and afterward thought of it constantly. She wanted him to own that Chardin, though admittedly he had finer pictures. In another letter, she made
a date with him to visit the Whitney Persian pottery
collection; she wanted to learn everything she could about
Persian art.

She advised him to go "South into the Sunshine," as it
would be good for him. She could not bear for him to be
worried and depressed and alone. She quoted verses by the
English statesman Lord Thomas Macaulay, written after
he had been defeated in an election, which she had kept
in her head for years. The verses described the consola-
tion he found in returning to "Literature" after his defeat.
"The Realm of Art" was also consoling, Mary Cassatt
wrote Stillman, and gave one serenity.

Again and again, she expressed her concern for his
health and happiness and her fear that he might be drawn
back into the "vortex of American business."

Late in 1910 the Gardner Cassatts arrived to take her
on an extensive journey to Munich, Constantinople, and
Egypt. Before they left Paris, Stillman took them all to the
Palace of Versailles and photographed them by the Grand
Trianon. Mary wrote him she was positive she had spoiled
the shot by her "absurd stiffness." She was always so afraid
of moving when she was photographed that she stood stiff
as a ramrod. She had not posed for years, but Joseph Durand-Ruel (the son of Paul Durand-Ruel) had made a
snapshot of her for publication—"a silly, simpering
thing," she dismissed it. At the age of sixty-six, Mary Cassatt retained a touch of feminine vanity.

She kept Stillman well informed of her trip with the
Gardner Cassatts. From Munich, she wrote complaining
that she had missed the city's most interesting sight—a

man 135 years old, in excellent health and enjoying all his faculties. From Constantinople (modern Istanbul), she reported that he might find that city more worth seeing than Naples or Venice. It was ideal for someone with a yacht; people subject to seasickness could sail on the smooth waters of its bay with pleasure. Back in Paris at last, she wrote that the last stage of their journey, in Egypt, had been a torture, but that one could learn to live "even on the rack." She had missed him dreadfully, she added, and would be ready for a drive at three that afternoon; she hoped they could see the Ingres exhibition together.

One reason Egypt had been such a strain for her was that Gardner was ill most of the time. He died in Paris on April 5, 1911. A memorial service was held for him in the English church in Paris. Mary Cassatt became enraged because the minister prayed for the king of England instead of the president of the United States. Though baptized an Episcopalian, she had never been much of a churchgoer and seems to have had little respect for religious ceremonies.

With the death of Gardner Cassatt, she became the only survivor among the family of five children who had made their first trip abroad in 1851. In a moment of depression she considered going home to America, but the dread of seasickness restrained her.

One day Stillman took his daughter-in-law Mildred to meet Mary at Beaufresne. Mildred described their hostess as "a tall gaunt woman" with a thin, strong face, erect body, and "swift hands," which she used to express her "mental vigor and vital interest in life." For dinner they had curried chicken, "a specialty of the house." The meal was punctuated with "Miss Cassatt's rapid intelligent conversation."

At some time in their relationship, Stillman suggested marriage. Mary Cassatt turned him down, doubtless encouraged by Mathilde Vallet, who said, "Surely, Mademoiselle, you would not adopt the name Stillman in place of Cassatt!"

While she refused to marry him, she paid him what no doubt in her mind was an even greater compliment. She offered to paint his portrait. He evaded the honor; the portrait was never made.

Her eyes had been troubling her off and on for some years. Because the shine on copper hurt them, she had to stop working on engravings. In 1912 she developed cataracts on both eyes. The subsequent operation was not wholly successful. A year later Stillman visited her at Grasse and found her morale high. She assured him she was now perfectly well and had gained sixteen pounds, but admitted that she was painting irregularly—only because it was hard to get models to come to her villa. She was eager to get back to Paris and to work.

He took her protestations with a grain of salt. To his sister he wrote that he was afraid if she went back to her old excitable life, she would learn that she had had a long illness and that she was not as young as she used to be. He admitted that neither he nor Mathilde Vallet nor anyone else could convince her to take it easy.

She was able to continue painting only about another year. Her last works, done as her sight was fading, show a marked deterioration and coarsening of technique. Sometime in 1914 she stopped painting altogether.

17

Tragic War Years

On August 2, 1914, the Germans crossed the French frontier, as Georges Clemenceau had been predicting they would do to his skeptical government colleagues. The First World War was launched. Parisians panicked, remembering the Siege of 1870. There was a mass exodus for the south. The government moved to Bordeaux.

At Beaufresne, in the war zone north of Paris, Mary Cassatt refused to budge until the military authorities brought pressure on her. She spent most of the war years in Grasse, with occasional visits to Paris, though she managed to wangle special permission from the military to return to Beaufresne for a few summers.

It was a dreary period for her. Her household staff was dispersed. Pierre Lefèbre, her chauffeur, was driving a car for a naval officer. Her gardener and his nineteen-year-old assistant were at the front. Mathilde Vallet, as an Alsatian, was considered an enemy alien; she left for Switzerland to work in a glove factory for the duration. Mary Cassatt had only a cook and a chambermaid to look after her. Her eyesight grew steadily worse. For the past several years she had dictated her correspondence to Mathilde. Now she had to write her own letters; her scrawl was almost illegible.

Life in France was a "sea of misery," she wrote Minnie, wife of her nephew Robert. "If only we could see the end of this war!" Casualties mounted horrendously. Before the end of the war, there would be more than 30 million dead, wounded, and missing, of which more than 6 million would be French soldiers, mostly young men. With at least 10,000 blind in the country—as she estimated it—Mary Cassatt accepted her own misfortune as of little importance.

She saw little of Stillman, who was engrossed in war work for his adopted country. During the first part of the war, he gave the French government half a million francs for war victims and another half a million francs for war orphans; organized and headed a New York committee to aid those French war orphans; and subscribed $20,000 to French war widows. His mansion on the rue de Rembrandt he turned over to the French government as a hospital for wounded officers. Stillman paid for modern medical equipment; left for the patients his furniture, pianos, games, and his well-stocked library; and supplied them with cigarettes, taxis, and champagne on their birthdays.

In August 1917 he left for America, where he died the following March after an illness of several months.

In November Mary Cassatt's old friend, Georges Clemenceau, now known as "The Tiger," was appointed Prime Minister for the second time. With a coalition cabinet he worked unceasingly for peace.

The only bright spot for Mary in the gloom of this terrible war was her visits to Renoir, who, feeble and ill as he was, still managed to make her laugh. As for Edgar Degas, the news she heard of him was devastating.

The last years had not dealt kindly with him. In 1912 his house on the rue Victor-Massé, where he had lived for thirty years, was sold over his head. A friend found him an apartment on the boulevard de Clichy, but the thought of leaving his familiar and cloistered surroundings horrified him. "What will become of me?" he demanded. That same year Henri Rouart died, the man who had been like a beloved brother to him.

The fear of blindness that had so long tortured him had become a reality. He, too, was losing his sight. When he could no longer see clearly enough to paint, he resumed sculpture, for which touch could replace sight. Although the results were brilliant, he told Ambroise Vollard sadly that he was taking up "a blind man's craft."

His old servant Zoë deserted him to take care of a niece. Another woman servant came to look after him, but she knew nothing of his habits and he was wretched. Unable to work, he walked endlessly and aimlessly through the streets of Paris, wearing an Inverness cape and a bowler hat green with age. His eyes became so bad he had to ask a policeman to help him cross the street. People compared him to King Lear. Mary Cassatt learned that he had taken to following funerals. She was distressed and shocked.

She visited him in Paris in 1917 and found him almost totally blind and confined to his bed. She knew he was pleased she was there, though he did not say so. Overcome with pity, she urged his niece, who was staying with him, to get a nurse for him. He died on September 27, 1917.

Mary Cassatt attended his funeral service in Montmartre with a few other of his old friends. A representative of President Poincaré came to throw a shovelful of earth on his grave. Otherwise his death passed almost unnoticed in the greater drama of the war.

In an almost indecipherable letter to the young dealer René Gimpel, Mary Cassatt wrote that she had seen Monet at the funeral. "I don't care for the water lilies; they seem to me like glorified wall paper." Monet's latest series, painted by his pool, was on water lilies. They enchanted almost everyone but Mary.

The first of four auctions of the contents of Degas' studio—the works of artists he admired and had collected and hoarded like a squirrel—was held in March 1918 (the same month that Stillman died in America) in the Georges Petit gallery. Bursting shells from the big German bombers made the glass roof vibrate during the bidding. The sale realized a total of 12 million gold francs, the Ingres and Delacroix paintings bringing the highest prices.

Mary Cassatt was back at the Villa Angeletto in Grasse at the time of the auction. René Gimpel came to see her there with his wife and two sons. They had hired a carriage and driver for the long, hard climb and still had to make the last lap of the journey on foot up a steep and narrow trail.

The villa was "perched on the mountain like a nest among branches," in Gimpel's words. There was a lovely view over the flower-fragrant countryside, but Mary Cassatt could no longer enjoy it. Although she had always loved flowers, her own garden was desolate.

Gimpel introduced her to his family, and she leaned over to peer more closely at his two sons, taking their heads in her hands. "How I should have loved to paint them," she said. He took it as a compliment since he knew she had always refused to do portraits of children who displeased her. She also expressed the hope that they "would live in a better world than ours."

They talked a long time—about the Degas sale; about Stillman's art collection; about Gauguin, whom she said she had never considered a painter; about Whistler, whom she termed "a talented mountebank," and Sargent, whom she dismissed as "a buffoon." But try as hard as he could, Gimpel could not make her talk about that fascinating period when she was a comrade and colleague of Degas, Manet, and the Impressionists.

Permission from the military authorities to return to Beaufresne for the summer came too late in 1918 for her to bother to make the trip. She was still in Grasse on November 11, 1918, when the armistice was signed and the world was again at peace.

18

A Remarkable Old Lady

Following the war, Mary Cassatt returned to Beaufresne, where she spent most of the rest of her life. Mathilde Vallet was back with her, as devoted as ever. A new chauffeur, Armand Delaporte, replaced Pierre Lefèbre. Her roses were as fragrant as ever.

Nothing shows her indomitable spirit better than the way she faced these last lonely years. Almost all the people who had been important to her were gone—her parents, her brothers and sister, Pissarro, Degas, Henry Have-

meyer, and James Stillman. Renoir, one of her last links
with the Impressionists, died on December 3, 1919. Only
Monet would outlive her, but much as she admired his
work, her friendship with him had never been very deep.
René Gimpel, on a visit to Giverny, informed him that
she was nearly blind, but he sensed "an old man's indifference" to her plight.

Operation after operation failed to improve her sight.
She suffered from diabetes and other ailments of old age.
Worst of all, she could no longer paint.

With all these heaping misfortunes, she remained un-
crushed. Instead of sinking into despair, she raged and
fumed. The Mary Cassatt people met in the postwar years
was opinionated, garrulous, and full of prejudices, but she
was always intensely alive, and as eloquent as ever in her
enthusiasms.

Her opinions, expressed forcefully, were neither logical
nor consistent. She advocated woman suffrage but opposed
women smoking; no female guest ever dared take a ciga-
rette in her home. Her moral standards were as inflexible
as ever. Visitors who did not strictly observe the proprie-
ties were never invited a second time. Yet she herself used
broad profanity to emphasize a point.

She detested the Germans, quoting the poet Schiller to
show how much they had changed since the eighteenth
century. In almost equally harsh terms she denounced
Woodrow Wilson for his share in the Treaty of Versailles.
Though she liked Georges Clemenceau as a person, she
declared she hated his politics. "The Tiger" was no longer
prime minister; his war reputation as savior of France had
not prevented a deluge of criticism from his opponents,
once the country was out of danger. The only politicians
who were not on Mary Cassatt's blacklist were the Social-
ists. "If I weren't a weak old woman I would throw away

my limousine, give up this apartment, and live without luxury," she said.

Her long-suppressed resentment against France and the French burst into the open. She insisted they were becoming immoral and worthless and advised American art students to study in their own country, not in "degenerate" France. The Latin Quarter of Paris was no place for a young lady to live alone, she scolded one female American art student.

So far as art was concerned, the clock had stopped for her with the death of Degas. The most modern artist she ever accepted was Cézanne, who was a precursor of the Cubists, in that he saw a painting as a composition of geometric forms. Even Cézanne never ranked with her three favorites—Degas, Manet, and Courbet. A Cézanne for which she originally paid 100 francs, she sold twenty-five years later for 8,000 francs, so she could buy a Courbet.

Cubism joined the long list of things and people against which and whom she had prejudices. As for the other new art movements—Post-Impressionism, Fauvism, Symbolism, Futurism, and the rest—she was hardly aware of their existence. Vollard once gave her several little terracotta statues. A friend asked her if they were by Aristide Maillol, but the name of this famous sculptor obviously meant nothing to her. Of Marie Laurencin's fanciful productions, she snapped, "I don't quite know what the world's coming to, if they call that painting."

Before Mary Cassatt's eyesight failed so badly, Mrs. Montgomery Sears took her to meet Gertrude Stein. With her brother, Leo, Miss Stein had begun an art collection with the purchase of a few Cézannes, and she enlarged it with works by Matisse, Picasso, and other *avant-garde* artists. She and Mary had in common not only their interest in art but their birthplace. Gertrude Stein, nearly thirty years the younger, had also been born in Allegheny City, Pennsylvania. But they never became friends. Mary stayed only briefly at the *soirée* and then asked Mrs. Sears to take her home. She had never in her life seen so many dreadful paintings, she commented, or seen so many dreadful people gathered in one place.

"No sound artist ever looked except with scorn at these cubists and Matisse," she wrote one of her nieces. (She would have been astounded at the veneration given to Henri Matisse in 1969, at the centenary celebration of his birth.) Gertrude Stein and her family had come to Paris "poor and unknown," she wrote in the same letter, then bought Matisse's pictures cheap and started to pose "as amateurs of the only real art."

This particular letter has several misstatements—Mary was under the impression that Leo was Gertrude Stein's husband—and it is also malicious to an uncalled-for degree. Yet there is no doubt that in her violent reaction, Mary Cassatt was completely in character. It was not only that most of Miss Stein's collection struck her as wild non-art. The very atmosphere of her salon was offensive to Mary's forthright nature. Ernest Hemingway and others have commented on the subservience the talented and domineering Gertrude Stein demanded of her coterie of artists and writers. With all her faults, Mary Cassatt had never demanded or received subservience from anyone. And she was a painter, while Gertrude Stein was not. It is no wonder that the clash of personalities of these two women, both strong-minded, made them irreconcilable.

Perhaps partly to snub France, and French artists, Mary professed a great interest in contemporary American art. Young expatriates were always welcomed to her home, where she served them tea, encouragement, advice, and criticism. She might not approve of their coming to

France at all, but once they were there, she did everything in her power to help them.

One of her most devoted followers among the younger generation of American artists was George Biddle of the Philadelphia Biddles, like herself a former student of the Pennsylvania Academy of the Fine Arts. Long before he knew her, his ambition was to paint as fine a picture as she or Edgar Degas had done. "The great artists of the past century—Degas, Millet, Delacroix, Mary Cassatt—all drew passionately," he wrote. He found such passion lacking among his contemporaries.

During the First World War, when Biddle was serving as an American soldier, he and a fellow artist, Abram Poole, bicycled to Beaufresne one Sunday. Mary Cassatt opened a bottle of old Burgundy for them, which she served with Philadelphia White Mountain Cake. How she got such luxuries in wartime remained a mystery. After the war Biddle continued to visit her, at Beaufresne or her Paris apartment, whenever he was in France. "If it is possible to love with a purely detached enthusiasm, then I loved this prim old Philadelphia lady," he wrote.

He never lost sight of Mary Cassatt, the artist, beneath her foibles of old age. Her mind "was neither balanced nor analytic" but "swept along enthusiastic and prejudiced. Like any artist's mind, good or bad, it saw things directly. . . . Her mind was great because it inspired others to see great truths, through her passion and single-mindedness."

Once Mathilde Vallet brought her mistress to a Paris exhibition of American art that George Biddle and his colleagues had organized. Mary admitted to him afterward that she could not see the paintings very distinctly: "It must have been a bad light." But Mathilde had led her to one of Biddle's works and she had made out that it was a still life, she told him. He was touched and flattered.

Another American admirer was Forbes Watson. As a youth he had seen one of Degas' etchings of Mary Cassatt at the Louvre. "The suggestion of grace, vigor, and smartness in the slender figure" had had a romantic appeal for him.

She did not resemble his image of her when he first met her at Beaufresne, but neither did she seem old. "There was in her, despite her lack of youth, an eagerness that made the years drop from her." Though her standards of good art did not embrace the new *avant-garde* movements, her artistic enthusiasms were still wide. "We must drive to Beauvais and see the windows that I love, the finest glass in all of northern France," she said after lunch.

Forbes Watson paid his last visit to her at her Paris apartment about eighteen months after the end of the war. She talked all day, mostly about politics. At five o'clock the maid served tea, with a large compote of strawberry jam. Miss Cassatt said, "If there is any jam on the table, help yourself." Startled, he realized for the first time that she was blind.

To another American artist, Adolphe Borie (also from the Pennsylvania Academy of the Fine Arts), she said, long after her own artistic career was over, "After all, woman's vocation in life is to bear children." The remark has been widely quoted as evidence that Mary Cassatt regretted not having led a normal married life with children of her own. Perhaps there were moments when she had such regrets—one cannot be sure. But it is hard to believe that if she had had her life to live over, she would have given up her career as an artist for that of a housewife.

Painting, like bearing children, is an act of creation. Mary Cassatt's children were her works of art. Just as one can consider her the mother of these products of her labor and love, one might also say that Degas fathered them. It was Degas, she would have been the first to admit, who transformed her from a competent artist into a superior one.

In her last years his name cropped up repeatedly whenever she talked of art. "No painter since Vermeer has mastered atmosphere the way he does," she said, speaking of him in the present tense, as though he were still living.

George Biddle once asked her if she would advise young artists to copy Rembrandt or Rubens. She shook her head. These two artists were finished masters; the purity of their line and design was hidden beneath the brilliancy of their technique. "Do you know what Degas said? One must enmesh oneself in the primitives."

Henri Matisse and other moderns were at that time "enmeshing themselves" in African art for inspiration. Perhaps Mary Cassatt did not know this. It was always, "Degas said . . ." She forgot many things in her old age, but what Degas had said about art was etched permanently on her consciousness.

Someone once got up the courage to ask if Degas had ever been her lover. She denied it emphatically and indignantly. Nothing matters less than whether she was telling the truth or what she now was convinced was the truth. On a purely artistic sphere, theirs was a great romance.

A distressing thing happened to her in 1923. Mathilde Vallet discovered twenty-five copper plates in a closet, all drypoints except two. Mary let a printer make nine prints of each of the twenty-five. He assured her they were of superb quality. Had she been able to see clearly, she would have been the first to criticize their unevenness and lack of sharpness. No one has ever been more exacting than she in insisting on clear, rich impressions.

Under the illusion that the plates had never before been printed, she sent on a set of the twenty-five to her lifelong friend Louisine Havemeyer, telling her to offer them to William M. Ivins, curator of prints at the Metropolitan Museum. Mr. Ivins saw at once that they were proofs drawn from worn-out plates. In fact, the Metropolitan already had good prints of most of them. Mrs. Havemeyer had the unpleasant task of writing to Mary Cassatt and telling her she had been deceived.

Mary would not believe her. Old, alone, and almost totally blind, she was convinced that her closest friend and Mr. Ivins were in league against her. In a series of indignant letters to Mrs. Havemeyer, she conjured up all manner of absurd and unjust accusations. The friendship that had meant so much to both of them was abruptly terminated, so far as Mary was concerned. To the end of her life, she would not admit that she was in the wrong.

In January 1926 George Biddle received a letter in her uncertain handwriting, inviting him to lunch at Beaufresne. In an accompanying note, Mathilde Vallet told him that her mistress had fallen from her bed several months before and could no longer walk unaided. He must not be shocked at her condition.

It was bitterly cold the day he arrived. Mathilde met him at the gate to tell him that Miss Cassatt had suffered a bad relapse. He ate alone, then Mathilde took him up to the artist's bedroom. Frail and emaciated and unseeing, her grey hair straggling from beneath her lace cap, she lay motionless on a big green bed. Yet once she began to talk, the very air seemed charged with her electric vitality.

Had he ever seen such terrible weather? she demanded. The doctor had told her it was the worst in forty years. She regretted that because of the weather she had been unable to join him at lunch. She hoped the bottle of Château Margaux was good; it was the last of a case of wine her brother Gardner had given her before his death . . . She intended to motor to Paris as soon as it was warmer.

"Her mind galloped along, shaking the frail human body," George Biddle would describe this last interview. At one point she spoke of the matter of the drypoint etchings, which Mrs. Havemeyer and the Metropolitan curator had said were faulty: "Such impudence!" She ordered Mathilde to bring in her lapis lazuli and carnelian Egyptian jewelry and spread it out on her bed to show him. Several times her memory failed her, and her face became tortured until Mathilde leaned over to supply the missing links in the conversation. At last she became exhausted and did not seem to notice when he left.

Less than six months later, on June 14, 1926, she died, resting on the arm of her chauffeur, Armand Delaporte. Since she had received the Legion of Honor, she was given an imposing funeral ceremony with military honors. The large attendance was mostly people of her neighborhood, for whom she had become an institution and a legend. There were many roses. She was buried in the Cassatt family vault at Mesnil-Théribus, next to her parents, her sister Lydia, and her brother Robert, who had died as a child in Germany and whose remains Mary had had brought back to France years before.

19

Aftermath

In May 1927 the Pennsylvania Museum held a Mary Cassatt exhibition, showing forty oils and pastels, more than a hundred prints, and fifteen watercolors and drawings. The museum bulletin carried a feature article about her and the exhibition by Mrs. Henry O. Havemeyer. "If ever there was a true artist, it was Mary Cassatt," wrote her forgiving friend.

As her bequest to the world, Mary left a total of some 225 prints and 940 paintings, pastels, and watercolors, according to Mrs. Adelyn Breeskin of the Smithsonian Institution, who has dedicated years of research to the preparation of *catalogues raisonnés*—complete catalogs—of her prints and her other works. It is a tremendous output, all the more impressive in view of her inflexible standards, the many sittings she demanded of her models, the infinite care she gave to everything she did.

Her work is still being rediscovered at frequent intervals in exhibitions held across the country. One of her mother-and-child paintings is in the White House. Almost every major museum in the country possesses some of her work. The Philadelphia Museum has six oil paintings, an assortment of drawings, nearly all her prints, and an impressive amount of information in its library about the life and works of this daughter of Philadelphia who became a great artist.

No one can now say that she is a prophet without honor in her own country. Except perhaps those who will never change.

At a gathering of Philadelphia high society—the society that once governed Mary Cassatt's own rigid moral standards—there was a debate as to the comparative merits of her work and the work of Cecilia Beaux, a talented but conventional artist from another distinguished Philadelphia family. In the midst of the discussion, when Mary seemed to be ahead, one person commented sourly, "But the Cassatts weren't really anybody!" The discussion closed with that.

Mary Cassatt's advice to her rich friends and relatives to buy works of her French colleagues as an *investment* has proved her a prophetess beyond anyone's expectation. Not only did Impressionist art increase in value many times during her lifetime. It has skyrocketed ever since.

Between 1950 and 1969, the prices of Renoirs alone increased more than 1,500 per cent. So dramatic has been the rise in Impressionist and other art categories, that it has been proposed that newspapers should publish art prices daily, alongside of stock quotations.

How would the artists have felt, had they been able to glimpse this brisk buying and selling, never to their benefit, often with the same spirit as that with which stocks and bonds are bought and sold? Renoir might have laughed. Sisley might have wept. Pissaro would have scowled at such commercialism. As for Mary Cassatt, she would probably have shrugged, or commented, as she did at her first favorable press notices: "Too much pudding!"

Partial List of Works by Mary Cassatt (Exclusive of Prints) in Major Museums

Baltimore, Maryland

BALTIMORE MUSEUM OF ART

"Augusta's Daughter and a Friend Seated Near a River Bank," watercolor   "Mother and Child," pastel

Boston, Massachusetts

MUSEUM OF FINE ARTS

"Mother and Child" (Caresse Maternelle), oil   "A Woman in Black at the Opera" (La Loge à l'Opéra), oil   "A Cup of Tea," oil   "Head of a Young Girl," oil   "Young Woman Reading" (Mrs. Duffee Seated on a

Striped Sofa, Reading), oil   "Two Sisters" (Study for
the Banjo Lesson), pastel   "Head of a Baby," pastel

Brooklyn, New York
BROOKLYN MUSEUM

"Mother and Child," oil   "Study of a Boy," watercolor
"La Toilette," pastel

Chicago, Illinois
ART INSTITUTE OF CHICAGO

"Woman Reading in a Garden" (Lydia Reading in a Garden; Femme Lisant), oil   "The Bath" (La Toilette de
l'Enfant), oil   "Mother Holding Child" (Sleepy Nicolle),
pastel   "Mother Adjusting Child's Bonnet," pastel

Cincinnati, Ohio
CINCINNATI ART MUSEUM

"The Loge," pastel   "Mother and Child" (Bébé en costume bleu, un doigt dans la bouche, dans les bras d'une
jeune femme en gris), oil

Cleveland, Ohio
CLEVELAND MUSEUM OF ART

"After the Bath," pastel   "Girl Seated," pencil   "Knitting in the Library," pencil   "The Letter," pencil

Detroit, Michigan
DETROIT INSTITUTE OF ART

"In the Garden," oil   "Women Admiring a Child," pastel

Hartford, Connecticut
WADSWORTH ATHENEUM

"Child Holding Dog," pastel   "Portrait of a Child,"
pencil

Newark, New Jersey
NEWARK MUSEUM

"Woman and Child" (Mathilde Vallet and Robert Cassatt), oil

New York City

METROPOLITAN MUSEUM OF ART

Oil Paintings

"Mother and Child"   "The Cup of Tea"   "Portrait of a Young Girl"   "Woman Sewing"   "Lady at the Tea Table"   "Mother and Boy"   "Young Mother Sewing"   "Lydia Cassatt Knitting in the Garden at Marly"   "Mrs. Robert Cassatt"   "Mother and Child"

Pastels

"Mother and Child" (five pastels of this title)   "Mother Feeding Her Child"   "Mother Playing with Her Child" "Child in Green Coat"   "Child in Orange Dress" "Master Gardner Cassatt and Miss Ellen Cassatt" "Woman on Bench"   "Ellen Mary Cassatt"   "Nurse and Child"   "Nurse Reading to a Little Girl"

Pencil on Paper

"Portrait of an Old Woman Knitting"   "Portrait of Child in Bonnet"   "Maternal Caress"   "Portrait Sketch"

Paris, France

THE LOUVRE

"Mère et Enfant" (Mother and Child), pastel   "Jeune Femme Cousant" (Young Woman Sewing), oil

Philadelphia, Pennsylvania

PENNSYLVANIA ACADEMY OF THE FINE ARTS

"Bacchante," oil

PHILADELPHIA MUSEUM OF ART

"During the Carnival" (Pendant le Carnaval), oil "Woman and Child Driving," oil   "In the Loge," oil "Alexander J. Cassatt and His Son, Robert Kelso Cassatt," oil   "Family Group Reading," oil   "Mother and Child Smiling at Each Other," oil   "Woman Arranging Her Veil," pastel

Pittsburgh, Pennsylvania

CARNEGIE INSTITUTE

"Young Women Picking Fruit," oil

San Diego, California

SAN DIEGO MUSEUM

"Young Girl in a Blue Bonnet," oil   "Sketch of a Girl," watercolor

Washington, D.C.

CORCORAN ART GALLERY

"Woman with a Dog" (Susan on a Balcony Holding a Dog; La Femme au Chien), oil

NATIONAL GALLERY OF ART

"The Boating Party" (La Partie en Bateau), oil   "The Loge" (Two Young Ladies in a Loge), oil   "Girl Arranging Her Hair" (La Toilette), oil   "Miss Mary Ellison" (Woman with a Fan), oil   "Mother and Child" "Portrait of an Elderly Lady," oil   "Woman Holding a Zinnia," oil

SMITHSONIAN INSTITUTION: NATIONAL COLLECTION
OF FINE ARTS

"The Caress" (Caresse Enfantine)   "Sara in a Green Bonnet" (La Filette au Chapeau Vert), oil

THE WHITE HOUSE

"Young Mother and Two Children," oil

Wichita, Kansas

WICHITA ART MUSEUM

"Mother and Child," oil

Bibliography

Bell, Clive. Introduction to *The French Impressionists in Full Colour*. New York: Phaidon Publishers, Inc., 1952.

Bernier, Georges and Rosamond, editors. *Modern Art Yesterday and Tomorrow*. New York: Reynal & Company, 1960.

Biddle, George. *An American Artist's Story*. Boston: Little, Brown and Company, 1939.

Bouret, Jean. *Degas*. New York: Tudor Publishing Company, 1965.

239

Breeskin, Adelyn D. Introduction to *The Graphic Art of Mary Cassatt*. New York: The Museum of Graphic Art with the Smithsonian Institution Press, 1967.

Breuning, Margaret. *Mary Cassatt*. New York: The Hyperion Press, 1944.

Burgess, George H., and Kennedy, Miles C. *Centennial History of the Pennsylvania Railroad Company 1846–1946*. Philadelphia: Pennsylvania Railroad Company, 1949.

Burr, Anna Robeson. *The Portrait of a Banker: James Stillman*. Cornwall, N.Y.: Cornwall Press, 1927.

Cabanne, Pierre. *The Great Collectors*. New York: Farrar, Straus, & Company, 1963.

Carson, Julia M. H. *Mary Cassatt*. New York: David McKay Company, Inc, 1966.

Chamson, André. *Gustave Courbet*. New York: Harry N. Abrams, Inc., 1957.

Fels, Florent. *Le Roman de L'Art Vivant—de Monet à Buffet*. Paris: Librairie Arthème Fayard, 1959.

Gimpel, René. *Diary of an Art Dealer*. New York: Farrar, Straus and Giroux, 1966.

Hamilton, George Heard. *Manet and His Critics*. New Haven: Yale University Press, 1954.

Hanson, Lawrence and Elisabeth. *Impressionism—Golden Decade 1872–1881*. New York: Holt, Rinehart and Winston, 1961.

Havemeyer, Louisine W. *Sixteen to Sixty—Memoirs of a Collector*. New York: Metropolitan Museum of Art, 1961.

Huyghe, René, general editor. *Larousse Encyclopedia of Modern Art*. New York: Prometheus Press, 1965.

Isham, Samuel. *The History of American Painting*. New York: The Macmillan Company, 1927.

Katz, Herbert and Marjorie. *Museums U.S.A.* New York: Doubleday & Company, Inc., 1965.

Martet, Jean. *Georges Clemenceau*. New York: Longmans Green and Company, 1930.

Mathey, François. *The Impressionists*. New York: Frederick A. Praeger, 1961.

Neilson, Winthrop and Frances. *Seven Women: Great Painters*. New York: Chilton Book Company, 1969.

Niess, Robert J. *Zola, Cézanne, and Manet—A Study of L'Oeuvre*. Ann Arbor: The University of Michigan Press, 1968.

Pissarro, Camille. *Letters to His Son Lucien,* edited by John Rewald with the assistance of Lucien Pissarro. New York: Pantheon Books, Inc., 1943.

Renoir, Jean. *Renoir, My Father*. Boston: Little, Brown and Company, 1958.

Rewald, John. *The History of Impressionism*. New York: The Museum of Modern Art, 1946.

Roger-Marx, Claude. *Les Impressionnistes*. Paris: Librairie Hachette, 1956.

Segard, Achille. *Un Peintre des Enfants et des Mères: Mary Cassatt*. Paris: 1913.

Sweet, Frederick A. *Miss Mary Cassatt: Impressionist from Pennsylvania*. Norman, Oklahoma: University of Oklahoma Press, 1966.

Venturi, Lionello. *Impressionists and Symbolists*. New York: Charles Scribner's Sons, 1950.

Vollard, Ambroise. *En Écoutant Cézanne, Degas, Renoir*. Paris: Bernard Grasset, 1938.

————. *Recollections of a Picture Dealer*. Boston: Little, Brown and Company, 1936.

Waleffe, Pierre, editor. *La Vie des Grands Peintres Impressionnistes*. Paris: Éditions du Sud, 1964.

Watson, Forbes. *Mary Cassatt*. American Artists Series. New York: Whitney Museum of American Art, 1932.

Weekes, C. P. *The Invincible Monet*. New York: Appleton-Century-Crofts, Inc., 1960.

Wilenski, R. H. *Modern French Painters*. New York: Harcourt, Brace & Company, 1949.

Index

243

About the Author

Robin McKown lived in France for several years, and there she came under the spell of French culture and taste. Her first research for THE WORLD OF MARY CASSATT was another visit to Paris, where she tried to view the City of Light as it must have seemed to Mary Cassatt when she first arrived from Philadelphia to study there nearly a century ago.

Mrs. McKown grew up in Denver and spent her summers in the tiny Rocky Mountain town of Ward, Colorado, altitude nine thousand feet, population thirty-seven. She was graduated from the University of Colorado and also studied at Northwestern University and the University of Illinois.

Mrs. McKown is the author of more than twenty-five books for young readers on such varied subjects as the French Resistance in World War II, Patrice Lumumba, atomic science, and the civilization of the Incas. Research for these books has taken her to many countries in Europe and Africa, but she now lives in western New York State, where her chief hobby is gardening. She writes that she has not yet rivaled Miss Cassatt's one thousand rosebushes, but she does enjoy the sixty which she recently planted.